Pre-Intermediate
Matters

GILLIE CUNNINGHAM

LONGMAN

Contents chart

Do you remember me?

GRAMMAR

Questions and answers

1 Read about Jeremy Guscott, the England rugby player and Jean-Paul Gaultier, the French fashion designer.

A   B

C   D

Jeremy Guscott

My wife Jayne and I wake up about 7 am when our two-year-old daughter Imogen gets up. My breakfast is always coffee, cornflakes and toast. I don't worry about the things I eat because I never get fat. I play rugby for Bath and England and work for the British Gas Company.

My office is a 15 minute drive from my home in Bath. I know I'm lucky to live in such a beautiful city. I would like to spend more time at home but in the rugby season (September to May) I train and exercise every evening and play matches every weekend. In the summer I travel for six to eight weeks with the Bath or England rugby team. Jayne and I don't go out very often in the evening because of Imogen, so friends visit us at home. The most important thing in my life is my family. Rugby comes second to that.

2 Which pictures show Jeremy's life? Which show Jean-Paul's?
Jeremy _____ Jean-Paul _____

3 Write questions for these answers. Use a word from the box to start each question.

When	Where	Who	How	What	Where

1 A: _____
    B: About 7 am.

2 A: _____
    B: She is Jeremy's daughter.

3 A: _____
    B: Coffee, cornflakes and toast.

4 A: _____
    B: He plays rugby matches.

5 A: _____
    B: He's a fashion designer.

6 A: _____
    B: He walks there from his flat.

7 A: _____
    B: In Pigalle, in central Paris.

8 A: _____
    B: After 1 am.

Jean-Paul Gaultier

I stay in bed one hour after I wake up. I know it's bad to do that. Then my housekeeper brings me my breakfast. I have carrot or orange juice, fruit salad, coffee with lots of milk and sugar and French bread with butter. At 10.30 I leave for my office – it's not a long walk from my flat in Pigalle. I love living in the centre of Paris.

I usually wear a T-shirt and jeans or trousers for work. I stay in the office until 8 pm and then I have dinner at home. At weekends, I like going to clubs to watch people dance. I don't drink very much alcohol but I talk a lot. It's always after 1 am when I go to bed.

(from *Radio Times*)

Subject and object questions

When *who* or *what* is the subject of a question, there is usually no auxiliary *do/does*. The words in the question are in the same order as a sentence.

Subject		Object
Gillian	likes	ice-cream.

Subject question A: *Who likes ice-cream?*
B: Gillian does.

Object question A: *What does Gillian like?*
B: Ice-cream.

4 Write subject and object questions for these answers.

1 Mary likes horror films.
 A: What _____ ?
 B: Horror films.
 A: Who _____ ?
 B: Mary does.

2 Jan drives an Italian car.
 A: Who _____ ?
 B: Jan does.
 A: What _____ ?
 B: An Italian car.

3 Simon has toast and coffee for breakfast.
 A: What _____ ?
 B: Toast and coffee.
 A: Who _____ ?
 B: Simon does.

Questions with *whose*

5 Complete the sentences.

1 A: Whose *coat is this?*/
  Whose *is this coat* _____ ?
 B: *It's* mine.

2 A: Whose _____ *shoes are these?*/
  Whose *are these shoes* _____ ?
 B: *They're* Joe's.

3 A: Whose _____ _____ ?
 B: _____ Gordon's.

4 A: Whose _____ _____ ?
 B: _____ Julia's.

5 A: Whose _____ _____ ?
 B: _____ Pat's.

6 A: Whose _____ _____ ?
 B: _____ Susan's.

7 A: Whose _____ _____ ?
 B: _____ Jane's.

8 A: Whose _____ _____ ?
 B: _____ Dan's.

VOCABULARY AND PRONUNCIATION

Nationalities and countries: word stress

6 a) Which is the stressed syllable in these nationalities? Find the correct stress pattern below. Use a dictionary to help you.

1 Peruvian _*B*_
2 Scottish _____
3 Russian _____
4 Argentinian _____
5 Egyptian _____
6 Spanish _____
7 Indian _____
8 Hungarian _____
9 Japanese _____
10 African _____
11 Austrian _____
12 American _____
13 Chinese _____
14 Brazilian _____
15 Italian _____

A	B	C	D	E	F	G
Ooo	oOoo	ooOoo	Oo	ooO	oO	oOo

b) [1.1] Listen and check your answers.

7 a) Write the country next to the nationality and mark the stressed syllable in each word.

	Nationality	Country
1	Japa'nese	_Ja'pan_
2	'German	_____
3	E'gyptian	_____
4	'Scottish	_____
5	I'talian	_____
6	Bra'zilian	_____
7	Hun'garian	_____

b) [1.2] Listen and check your answers.

8 Are the underlined words correct? If not, write the correct word.

1 Is there a <u>Hungary</u> student here? ✗ *Hungarian*
2 I come from <u>England</u>. ✓ _____
3 He always wears <u>Italy</u> suits. _____
4 They speak <u>Spanish</u> in Argentina. _____
5 Morocco is in north <u>African</u>. _____
6 A Volkswagen is a <u>Germany</u> car. _____
7 Is Bruce from <u>Scottish</u>? _____
8 Are they <u>Brazilian</u>? _____

LISTENING

9 [▭ 1.3] Look at Sue's student card. Some of the information on it is wrong. Listen to her conversation in the university canteen and correct the wrong information.

WESTMINSTER UNIVERSITY
STUDENT INFORMATION

First name *Sue*
Surname *Bernet*
Course *Computer Studies*
Room *12 L*
Starting Date *10 October*
Time *8.30 am*

Why did you choose this course? *In the future I want to work for a big computer company like Apple Macintosh.*

WRITING

Punctuation

10 Rewrite these sentences using capital letters (***America***), full stops (**.**), commas (**,**) and question marks (**?**).

1 peter starts his new job on 1 May
  Peter starts his new job on 1 May. _____

2 julia travels to france brazil america and spain every year
  _____

3 your plane leaves on monday at 18.00 hours and you arrive in madrid at 20.00 hours
  _____

4 I want to leave at about 7.45 tomorrow morning can you wake me up at 6 o o'clock
  _____

5 my next dentist's appointment is at 2.15 pm on tuesday 30 september
  _____

6 when is amybeth's birthday it's on 21 december
  _____

DICTATION

Dates and times

11 [▭ 1.4] Listen to the cassette. Some of the information in the sentences above is wrong. Write the correct sentences from the cassette.

1 *Peter starts his job on 31 May.*
  NOTE We say: 'the thirty-first of May'. We write: 31 May.

2 _____
3 _____
4 _____
5 _____
6 _____

Spend, spend, spend!

GRAMMAR

Present Continuous or Present Simple?

1 It is Monday at the office. Peter and Sam are talking about Simon. Complete their conversations with the correct form of the verbs in brackets.

1 PETER: What's the matter with Simon? He usually (*come*) <u>comes</u> to work in jeans and a T-shirt.

   SAM: Oh, yes! He (*wear*) <u>'s wearing</u> his best suit.

2 PETER: What's the matter with Simon? He (*smile*) _____ and he's happy.

   SAM: That's unusual for Simon. He's usually so angry on a Monday morning. He always (*shout*) _____ at everyone on Mondays!

3 PETER: What's the matter with Simon? Look, he (*have*) _____ lunch in the office cafeteria!

   SAM: Yes he is! He (*not eat*) _____ here very often, does he? He usually (*go*) _____ out for lunch.

4 PETER: What's the matter with Simon? It's after 5 o'clock, and he (*work*) _____ !

   SAM: But he never (*work*) _____ this late! He's always the first person to leave the office.

5 PETER: Look over there. Who (*Simon/talk*) _____ to?

   SAM: Oh, that's the **new** art director, Sally.

   PETER: Oh, that's what's the matter with Simon! He's in love again.

   SAM: Yes. He always (*fall*) _____ in love with new women in the office. But poor Simon, they never fall in love with him!

Short answers

2 Answer these questions about Simon. Use short answers.

1 A: Is Simon wearing jeans?
   B: <u>No, he isn't.</u>

2 A: Does he usually wear jeans?
   B: <u>Yes, he does.</u>

3 A: Does Simon usually come to work in a suit?
   B: _____

4 A: Does Simon often eat in the office cafeteria?
   B: _____

5 A: It's after five o'clock. Is Simon still working?
   B: _____

6 A: Does Simon usually leave work at 5 pm?
   B: _____

7 A: Is Simon talking to the manager?
   B: _____

Question forms

3 a) Put these words in the correct order to make questions.

1 time/usually/do/what/finish/you/work?

What time do you usually finish work?

2 Sam/Jane/now/are/living/where/and?

_____

_____

3 sell/you/stamps/do?

_____

_____

4 always/they/do/wine/meals/drink/with/their?

_____

_____

5 the/does/close/bank/when?

_____

6 often/Pamela/does/tennis/weekends/the/play/at?

_____

_____

7 noise/who/that/making/is?

_____

b) Match these answers with the questions above.

a) Yes. Would you like first or second class? *3*

b) Yes, she does in the summer, but not in the winter. ___

c) Somewhere near Edinburgh in Scotland. ___

d) Oh, it's the children. They're playing football. ___

e) I'm not sure. I think it's 4.30, but they are open on Saturday mornings. ___

f) No. Only when they have dinner parties. ___

g) Usually at about six. ___

Frequency adverbs

October							November						
S	M	T	W	T	F	S	S	M	T	W	T	F	S

October

S M T W T F S

1 2 3 4 5 6

7 8 9 10 11 12 13

14 15 16 17 18 19 20

21 22 23 24 25 26 27

28 29 30 31 Swimming Tennis Tennis

Swimming Tennis Tennis Tennis

November

S M T W T F S

1 2 3

4 5 6 7 8 9 10

11 12 13 14 15 16 17

18 19 20 21 22 23 24

25 26 27 28 29 30 Tennis

Swimming Tennis Tennis Swimming Tennis

4 Look at Janet's calendar for October and November. Use the words below to make sentences about Janet.

never   rarely   sometimes   often   usually   always
0% ◄——+——+——+——► 100%

1 Janet *never plays* tennis on Sundays.

2 Janet _____ tennis on Mondays.

3 Janet _____ tennis on Tuesdays.

4 Janet _____ tennis on Wednesdays.

5 Janet _____ tennis on Thursdays but she _____ swimming.

6 Janet _____ tennis on Fridays.

7 Janet _____ tennis on Saturdays.

8 Janet _____ tennis on Sundays but she _____ swimming.

VOCABULARY

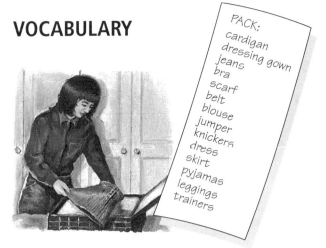

PACK:
cardigan
dressing gown
jeans
bra
scarf
belt
blouse
jumper
knickers
dress
skirt
pyjamas
leggings
trainers

5 Look at the pictures. Rebecca packed these things last night. Look at her list. Which five things did she NOT put in her suitcase last night?

1 _____

2 _____

3 _____

4 _____

5 _____

6 [🎞 2.1] Listen. Where would you hear these sentences? Match the sentences with the places.

1 Have you got these boots in black?

2 I'd like a kilo of sausages, please.

3 Could I have soup of the day, please, and a coffee?

4 I'd like to change ten pounds into dollars, please.

5 Can I have two kilos of white grapes, please?

6 May I have a large white loaf and four of those cakes, please?

7 Can I try this sweatshirt on, please?

a) restaurant _3_   e) clothes shop ___

b) greengrocer's ___   f) bank ___

c) butcher's ___   g) shoe shop ___

d) baker's ___

READING

A *My jeans, definitely. They are very easy to wear. I wear them with a sweatshirt or a T-shirt. I bought them about four years ago. They were quite expensive but they fit me perfectly. When I'm modelling all day, I always go home and put them on immediately.*

B **Yes. Modelling agencies always tell models they must look good and wear smart clothes, but it's quite difficult at the beginning of your career. You don't have much money and good clothes aren't usually cheap. I know a lot of models who borrow money so they can look really good all the time. But I don't think it's a great idea to begin your career by having problems with money.**

C *My leather trousers are very special. I bought them with the money I earned from my first modelling job. I wore them all the time because I loved them so much. But then I lost a bit of weight, so they don't fit me any more. I'll always keep them though.*

D **I don't do anything special. I have a quick shower, wash my face and dry my hair. I only wear make-up when I'm working, so I can be out of the house in twenty minutes.**

E *Yes, I've got a horrible yellow T-shirt. I liked it when I bought it. It wasn't new – it was second-hand. I think I liked it because it was a designer T-shirt and very cheap. It makes me look ill, so I never wear it any more.*

7 Sacha is a model. She's talking about her clothes. Read the paragraphs and match them with these questions.

1 Is it important for models always to wear stylish clothes? _B_

2 Do you usually spend a lot of time getting ready to go out? ____

3 What's your favourite item of clothing? ____

4 Have you got any clothes you really don't like? ____

5 What's your most comfortable item of clothing? ____

8 Read the article again. Write *True* (T) or *False* (F) next to these sentences.

1 Sacha only buys new clothes. __*F*__

2 Sacha only wears really smart clothes now._____

3 Sacha thinks really good clothes are usually expensive._____

4 When she started modelling, Sacha didn't borrow money to buy nice clothes._____

5 Sacha doesn't spend a lot of time on her hair._____

6 She doesn't wear her leather trousers now because they look old._____

7 Sacha bought the yellow T-shirt because the colour yellow looks good on her._____

WRITING

Spelling

9 Write the third person of the Present Simple of these verbs.

	Present Simple third person
1 watch	*watches*
2 go	_____
3 play	_____
4 buy	_____
5 carry	_____
6 do	_____
7 wash	_____
8 sell	_____
9 wear	_____
10 fly	_____
11 write	_____

10 Write the *-ing* form of these verbs.

	-ing **form**
1 sit	*sitting*
2 run	_____
3 drive	_____
4 go	_____
5 fly	_____
6 take	_____
7 play	_____
8 come	_____
9 swim	_____
10 stop	_____
11 have	_____

PRONUNCIATION

Sound and spelling / ə /

11 a) Which of the underlined letters has the weak sound /ə/?

1 pyjamas	*pyjamas*	7 summer	_____
2 American	_____	8 trainers	_____
3 Brazilian	_____	9 police	_____
4 again	_____	10 often	_____
5 picture	_____	11 Japanese	_____
6 mother	_____	12 cardigan	_____

b) [2.2] Listen and check your answers. Practise saying the words.

DICTATION

Vocabulary

12 [2.3] Rebecca and Clare are sisters. They're on holiday. Listen and complete their conversation.

CLARE: Rebecca, someone has stolen *my suitcase*!

REBECCA: No! Are you sure?

CLARE: Yes. _____ not in _____ _____.

REBECCA: What was in it?

CLARE: _____ of my _____. I started to unpack my suitcase _____ _____ but I was _____ so I didn't _____.

REBECCA: Well, what do you need? I've got extra _____ and _____ and _____.

CLARE: Have you got an extra _____ _____?

REBECCA: No. But can't you wear _____ and a _____ to swim in?

CLARE: No, I can't but I've got some _____. I can buy _____.

REBECCA: What clothes have you got?

CLARE: What I'm wearing: my _____ and this _____. Erm ... my _____, my _____ _____ and the _____ and _____ I wore on the plane.

REBECCA: OK. We can go to the _____ now, buy you a swimming costume and then go to the beach.

The family unit

GRAMMAR

Present Simple or Past Simple?

1 Complete the sentences with verbs from the box in the correct form.

work   sleep   phone   be   play   study   watch   get up   finish

1 Jack usually _works_ until 7.30, but last night he _finished_ early.
2 Paula usually _____ golf on Fridays, but last Friday she _____ squash with Jonathan.
3 Sam and Sarah usually _____ at 8 am, but yesterday they _____ until lunchtime.
4 Daniel usually _____ his mother once a week, but last week he _____ her every evening because she _____ ill.
5 I usually _____ in the evenings, but last night I _____ a great film on TV.

Past Simple or Past Continuous?

2 a) Read Tom's story. Circle the correct form of the verb.

Me and my brother Ben

I like my brother now, but I (1) _didn't like_ / wasn't liking him when we were children. He (2) _did/was doing_ some really terrible things to me. One day we (3) _played/were playing_ in the park when it (4) _began/was beginning_ to rain. My brother (5) _wanted/was wanting_ my bike, but I said no. I (6) _got/was getting_ on my bike and while I (7) _rode/was riding_ along the path, he (8) _threw/was throwing_ his coat over my face and I (9) _fell/ was falling_ off my bike and (10) _cut/was cutting_ my knees. I (11) _left/was leaving_ my bike in the park and I (12) _ran/was running_ home to tell my mother. When I (13) _found/was finding_ her, she (14) _talked/was talking_ to our neighbour Mr Jones in the garden. She (15) _told/was telling_ Mr Jones that my brother and I were good friends. When I (16) _told/was telling_ her what (17) _was happening/happened_ in the park, she (18) _said/was saying_ to Mr Jones, 'Well, they were friends yesterday!'

b) [🔊 3.1]   Listen and check your answers.

3 Write the correct form of the verb in brackets.

1 While we (_walk_) _were walking_ in the park my Aunt (_fall_) _fell_ in the river!
2 When I (_see_) _____ John, he (_talk_) _____ to the manager.
3 Sarah and Jack (_watch_) _____ TV when I (_arrive_) _____.
4 While Corrine (_not look_) _____ , her daughter (_run_) _____ into the road.
5 I (_study_) _____ when my sister (_phone_) _____.

Prepositions of time

4 Complete these sentences with the correct prepositions where necessary.

1 I'm going on holiday _X_ next week. I'm flying to Ankara _on_ Monday morning.
2 What are you going to do __ your birthday?
3 My grandmother was born __ the nineteenth century, and she died __ 1925.
4 I start my new job __ nine o'clock __ Tuesday.
5 What did you do __ last night?
6 What do you do __ the evenings, after work?
7 My grandmother always has a little sleep __ the afternoon.

VOCABULARY

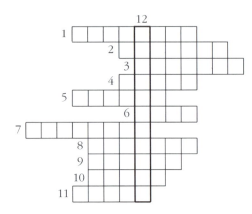

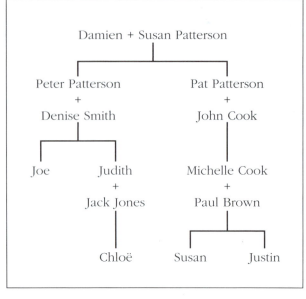

5 Complete the word puzzle. All the words are from Units 1–3 in the Students' Book.

1 A person from Japan is _____.

2 A person from Mexico is _____.

3 The name of a famous Spanish artist.

4 Men often wear a _____ and tie.

5 You wear these on your hands.

6 Husband and _____.

7 It's like a jumper, but it opens and has buttons.

8 A person who doesn't get angry when you are late is _____.

9 A person who never tells lies is _____.

10 Opposite of *white*

11 My father's brother is my _____.

What are the two family members in the centre box?

12 _____

6 Look at the family tree.

1 Who am I?
That's Michelle, she's my cousin.
That's my grandfather. Damien Patterson.
That's my Aunt Pat.
That's my niece Chloë.
I am _____.

Now you know my name, complete these sentences about my family.

2 Judith is my _____.

3 Susan Patterson is my _____.

4 John Cook is my _____.

5 John Cook is my mother's _____.

6 Michelle is Damien Patterson's _____.

LISTENING

YOUR POSITION IN THE FAMILY IS IMPORTANT TO YOUR PERSONALITY

7 Before you listen, think about these questions.

1 What is your position in your family? Are you the oldest/middle/youngest child? Are you an only child?

2 Do you think a child's position in the family is important to his/her personality?

8 a) Read the information about Anne, Brian and Gillian.

Anne Lombard
1 Age: <u>27</u>
2 Position in the family: <u>the youngest</u>
3 Anne's sister is <u>fun-loving.</u>
4 Anne's brother is <u>friendly and fun-loving.</u>
5 Anne is <u>serious.</u>

Brian Tellerman
1 Age: <u>33</u>
2 Position in the family: <u>the oldest</u>
3 Brian is <u>generous and fun-loving.</u>

Gillian Whitefield
1 Age: <u>we don't know</u>
2 Position in the family: <u>the oldest</u>
3 Her brother <u>likes being alone.</u>
4 Gillian's sister is often <u>angry.</u>
5 Gillian is <u>serious.</u>

b) [3.2] Some of the information is wrong. Listen and correct the wrong information.

WRITING

Linking words

9 Use one of the linking words in the box to complete the sentences.

> and   but   so   because

1 This morning I bought some milk <u>*and*</u> some bread.
2 I got a pen for my birthday _____ I wanted a dictionary.
3 I didn't have any cash _____ I went to the bank.
4 I went to the bank _____ I didn't have any cash.

5 I wanted to go to the party _____ I was very tired.
6 I was very tired _____ I didn't go to the party.
7 My aunt _____ my uncle went to the theatre last night.
8 I went to the doctor's _____ I had a bad cough.
9 I had a bad cough _____ I went to the doctor's.

DICTATION

Pronunciation

10 a) [3.3] Listen and complete these sentences with contracted forms where possible.
1 Jane's got <u>*a*</u> new boyfriend. His <u>*name's*</u> Peter.
2 _____ like _____ bottle _____ shampoo _____ _____ toothbrush, please.
3 _____ buying _____ present _____ their mother.
4 I like walking. I _____ need _____ car.
5 She _____ want _____ cup _____ coffee.
6 _____ got _____ letter _____ Jennifer.

b) Listen again. Circle the word with the most stress in each sentence.

Giving personal information

11 [3.4] Listen and complete the sentences with information about your life.

Dictation	You
1 *I was born on*	_____
2	_____
3	_____
4	_____
5	_____

Me and my body

GRAMMAR

Permission: *can* and *can't*

1 Janet is going to university in London next month, and she needs somewhere to live. Her friend told her about Mrs Jones who has a room to rent.

These are Mrs Jones' rules for people who live in her house.

```
                    HOUSE RULES
        ✓                            ✗
bicycles in the garage       bicycles in the hall
smoke in your bedroom        smoke in the kitchen
use the kitchen until 10 pm  pets in the house
have visitors until 11 pm
use the phone
```

a) What questions did Janet ask Mrs Jones?

1 JANET: *Can I smoke in the house?*

MRS JONES: Well, you can smoke in your room, but you can't smoke in the kitchen.

2 JANET: _____?

MRS JONES: Yes, you can, but you have to pay for the calls you make.

3 JANET: _____?

MRS JONES: Yes, you can, but not after 11 pm.

4 JANET: _____?

MRS JONES: No, I'm sorry you can't. I don't want animals in the house.

5 JANET: _____?

MRS JONES: Yes, you can, but not after 10 pm.

6 JANET: _____?

MRS JONES: Yes, you can, but you must keep it in the garage.

b) Mrs Jones saw Janet:

- smoking in the kitchen
- bringing a cat into the house
- talking to friends in her room at midnight
- cooking at 1 am
- putting her bicycle in the hall

What did Mrs Jones say to Janet?

1 *You can't smoke in the kitchen.* _____

2 _____

3 _____

4 _____

5 _____

Obligation and advice

leave out. 30.11.98

✗ **2** Circle the best verb for these sentences.

1 It's very early. We *must/don't have to* leave now.
2 We can go to the cinema tonight. I *must/ don't have to* work.
3 You look tired. You *should/mustn't* have a holiday.
4 That's a great film. You *don't have to/must* see it.
5 This letter isn't important. You *don't have to/ must* send a reply.
6 His leg is broken. We *should/must* phone the doctor.
7 It's very late. The film starts in five minutes. We *must/don't have to* leave now.

Can/could/may/would

3 Which sentence is grammatically correct?

1 a) Please would I use your phone? ✗
  b) Please may I use your phone? ✓

2 a) Would you like a cup of coffee? ___
  b) Would you liking a cup of coffee? ___

3 a) May you help me, please? ___
  b) Can you help me, please? ___

4 a) Could I borrow your pen, please? ___
  b) Could I to borrow your pen, please? ___

5 a) Can you to drive? ___
  b) Can you drive? ___

6 a) Please may you open the window for me? ___
  b) Please would you open the window for me? ___

VOCABULARY

Clothes and jewellery

4 Match the words in the box with the pictures.

| earrings   trousers   ring   belt   watch   trainers   gloves |

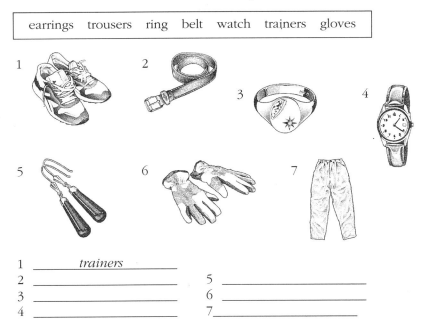

1 _____trainers_____
2 _____ 5 _____
3 _____ 6 _____
4 _____ 7 _____

Parts of the body, clothes and jewellery

5 What clothes and jewellery do you wear on these parts of your body? More than one word may be possible for each picture.

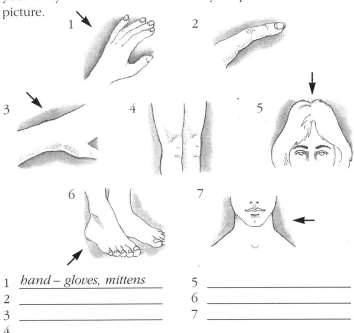

1 _hand – gloves, mittens_ 5 _____
2 _____ 6 _____
3 _____ 7 _____
4 _____

You need a doctor!

6 Complete the sentences with words from the box.

twisted   feet hurt   ached   cough   sore throat   vitamins   felt   headache

1 Yesterday I had a _headache_ so I took an aspirin.

2 Last week I had a _____ so I bought some lozenges.

3 Last month I _____ my knee and I went to the hospital for an X-ray.

4 My back _____ all morning so I went to bed.

5 I _____ awful all day yesterday so I didn't go to work.

6 I didn't want to catch a cold so I took _____ every day in the winter.

7 I've got a really bad _____ so the doctor gave me some medicine.

8 My _____. My new shoes are too small.

LISTENING

7 Make a list of things that you like about your body and things you don't like about your body on a separate piece of paper.

8 [📼 4:1] Listen to Mike and Debbie talking about things they like and don't like about their bodies.

a) Look at Mike and Debbie's lists. Put a ✗ next to the parts of the body they don't like. Put a ✔ next to the parts of the body they like.

b) Do they talk about any of the things you have on your list?

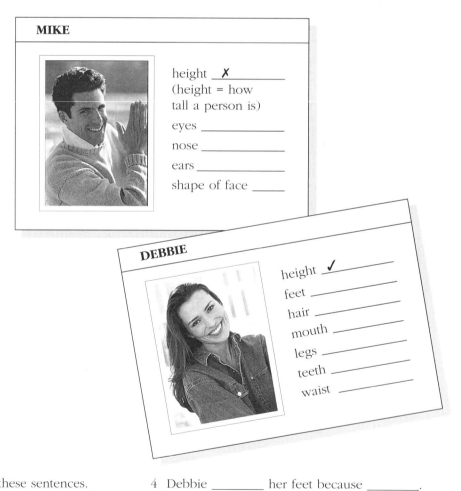

MIKE

height __✗_____
(height = how tall a person is)

eyes _____

nose _____

ears _____

shape of face _____

DEBBIE

height __✔_____

feet _____

hair _____

mouth _____

legs _____

teeth _____

waist _____

c) Listen again and complete these sentences.

1 Debbie _likes_ her legs because _they're long_.

2 Debbie _doesn't like_ her mouth because _it's big_.

3 Mike _____ his nose because _____.

4 Debbie _____ her feet because _____.

5 Mike _____ his ears because _____.

4 Debbie _____ her feet because _____.

5 Mike _____ his ears because _____.

6 Debbie _____ her hair because _____.

7 Debbie _____ her waist because _____.

WRITING

Spelling

9 a) Complete this postcard with one of the linking words in the box.

> and   but   because

I'm writing this on my balcony with a cold drink on a hot, hot day! My room is cheep (1) _and_ comfortable. Life is good. This is a really beutiful (2) _____ intresting island (3) _____ there's a lot to see. Everyday they put fresh flowers on the streets. This makes everything look very atractive. The weather is always suny, (4) _____ I have to be carefull (5) _____ I get sunburnt very quickly. There are only two problems. One is I'm getting fat (6) _____ the food is really dilicious, (7) _____ the other is I don't want to leave!

        Love
        Penny

b) There are eight spelling mistakes on the postcard. They are all adjectives. Find the mistakes and correct the spellings.

1 _____   4 _____   7 _____
2 _____   5 _____   8 _____
3 _____   6 _____

DICTATION

Sound and spelling /iː /

10 a) [🔊 4.2]   Listen and complete the sentences.

1 _____ _____'s very _____, the food's great and I'm _____ a lot.
2 I'm _____ for London next _____.
3 I _____ _____ stop. My _____ _____ hurting.
4 I _____ _____ today.
5 _____ _____ sentences.
6 _____ _____ lots of _____ on _____ bus.
7 My _____ is _____ tomorrow.

b) Listen again and underline the words with the sound /iː/. Practise saying these words.

c) The sound /iː/ has different spellings. Put the words you have underlined in the correct place on the table.

ie	
ee	
ea	
eo	
ete	*complete*
ese	

Getting around

GRAMMAR

Will or *going to* ?

1 Complete these conversations. Use <u>*will*</u> or <u>*going to*</u> with the verbs in brackets.

1 DAVE: Can you help me this evening, Simone? I really must finish this report.

  SIMONE: Oh, I'm sorry Dave, I can't. I (*visit*) (1) <u>*'m going to visit*</u> Jane in hospital.

  DAVE: Jane's in hospital! I didn't know. What's wrong?

  SIMONE: She (*have*) (2) _____ an operation on her foot.

  DAVE: Oh, dear! That sounds bad. I (*buy*) (3) _____ her some magazines and chocolates.
Can you take them to her for me? I have to work this evening.

  SIMONE: Yes, OK. I (*leave*) (4) _____ the office about six. Can you give them to me before then?

  DAVE: Yes, I can. I (*bring*) (5) _____ them to your office. Thanks Simone.

2 SIMONE: Have you seen Richard Gere's new film?

  DAVE: No. Is it good?

  SIMONE: Yes. It's fantastic!

  DAVE: I'm free this weekend. I (*go*) _____ and see it on Saturday.

3 DAVE: Do you want to come to the pub for a drink?

  SIMONE: I can't. I haven't got any money with me.

  DAVE: No problem. I (*buy*) (1) _____ you a drink.

  SIMONE: Great, and I (*give*) (2)_____ you the money back tomorrow.

4 SIMONE: Pete (*get*) (1) _____ a new job. Did you know?

  DAVE: No, I didn't. Who (*work*) (2) _____ he _____ for?

  SIMONE: I can't remember. I (*ask*) (3) _____ Pat. She knows everything about this office.

Will for offers, requests and decisions at the moment of speaking

2 a) Match a sentence from A with an answer from B.

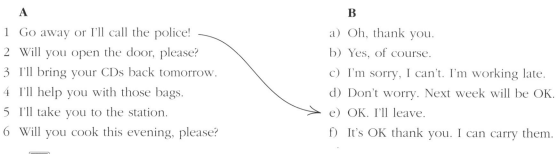

A

1 Go away or I'll call the police!

2 Will you open the door, please?

3 I'll bring your CDs back tomorrow.

4 I'll help you with those bags.

5 I'll take you to the station.

6 Will you cook this evening, please?

B

a) Oh, thank you.

b) Yes, of course.

c) I'm sorry, I can't. I'm working late.

d) Don't worry. Next week will be OK.

e) OK. I'll leave.

f) It's OK thank you. I can carry them.

b) [5.1]   Listen and check your answers.

Future time using *will, going to* or the Present Continuous

Selling my car?

Buying a bicycle?

3 a) Circle the best form of the verb for these sentences.

1 DAN: I've decided to help the environment! I (*am going to sell*/*will sell*) my car and get a bicycle.

2 SUE: Oh. Good idea. But you can't ride a bicycle to work. It's fifty kilometres. How are you (*going to get*/*getting*) there?

3 DAN: Good question. I hate buses. I think I (*am taking*/*will take*) the train.

   SUE: How much do you want for the car?

4 DAN: I'm not sure. It isn't new. It's five years old now. I think I (*will ask*/*am asking*) for £999.50!

5 SUE: Well, I (*am going to buy*/*will buy*) it for that price. And I (*am giving*/*will give*) you an extra 50 pence to make it a £1000.

   DAN: Great! Ah, another idea. You can drive me to work.

   SUE: What about the environment?

6 DAN: Yes, but it (*is not being*/*won't be*) my car!

   b) [🎞 5.2]   Listen and check your answers.

Will for offers and requests

4 Use the verbs in brackets to make offers and requests.

1 You want Jim to open the window.
   (request/*open*)   *Will you open the window please, Jim?*

2 David needs help with his English homework.
   (offer/*help*)   *I'll help you with your homework, David.*

3 You want to get a taxi home, but you haven't got any money.
   (request/*lend*)   _____

4 An old man is carrying a heavy bag.
   (offer/*carry*)   _____

5 Your friend can't find a taxi to take him to the station.
   (offer/*take*)   _____

6 You're in the office and it's dark. Penny is near the light switch.
   (request/*switch on*)   _____

7 Your friend is thirsty. She likes coffee.
   (offer/*make*)   _____

VOCABULARY

5 The words in the box have similar meanings, but we use them in different ways. Write the correct word in each sentence in the correct form. Use your dictionary to help you.

> trip (*noun*)   journey (*noun*)
> travel (*uncountable noun or verb*)

1 I want to *travel* a lot when I leave university.

2 We're going on a coach _____ tomorrow to see where President Kennedy lived.

3 It was such a long train _____. It took eight hours.

4 Are you _____ by car or by train?

5 Are you going on the school _____ to Cambridge tomorrow?

6 Put the words in the box in the correct place in the table.

| to land   a cruise   a windscreen   a cabin |
| to take off   to sail   a brake   to brake |
| traffic lights   stop sign   seat belt (x2) |
| boarding card (x2)   to drive   to fly |

Travelling by:

	a cruise	

7 Choose a word which has the opposite meaning of the underlined word. Then complete the sentences.

| safe   wet   full   cheap   noisy |

1 A: Flying is very <u>dangerous</u>

   B: No, flying is very *safe* .

2 A: Your children are very <u>quiet</u>.

   B: They're usually very _____!

3 A: Is your hair <u>dry</u> now?

   B: No, it's still _____.

4 A: I've eaten a lot and I'm still <u>hungry</u>.

   B: Oh, I'm not. I'm really _____.

5 A: I need a new pen, but this is <u>expensive</u>.

   B: There's a _____ one, over there.

READING

8 Sue Daniels works in Camden, in North London. She drives to work each day.

a) Before you read the article, think about these questions.

1 Do you live in a town, a city or a village?

2 Is there a lot of traffic where you live?

3 Is it easy to find a place to park?

4 What happens if you park in the wrong place?

b) Now read this article from a newspaper.

An expensive place to park

It's nearly impossible to find a place to park in London. And when you can find a place to park in <u>this city</u>, is it safe? It wasn't for Sue Daniels.

   Sue Daniels works for a TV company in Camden in London. Yesterday morning she parked her car on a road that didn't have any parking meters on <u>it</u>. Eleven hours later, when she returned to her car there was a parking meter next to <u>it</u>. She had a parking ticket and someone had clamped the wheels on her car, so she couldn't drive home.   5   10

   'I couldn't believe it!' she said. 'I didn't know they planned to put parking meters on that road. There weren't any notices <u>there</u> about new parking meters. I had to pay £58 before I could drive home!'   15

   However, she got her money back from the Parking Ticket Office in Camden, and <u>they</u> apologised. 'We don't usually start using the parking meters until the next day,' said a man from the office. 'It was a mistake, and we are sorry.' (from *The Evening Standard*)   20

9 These sentences give the wrong information. Correct the information as in the example.

1 It's easy to park in London.

   No, it isn't. It's difficult to park in London.

2 Sue Daniels works for the Parking Ticket Office in Camden.

   _____

3 In the morning she parked her car next to a parking meter.

   _____

4 After work she got in her car and drove home.

   _____

5 She had to pay £50 before she could drive home.

   _____

10 What do the underlined words in the article refer to?

1 this city (line 3)   = *London*
2 it (line 8)   = _____
3 it (line 10)   = _____
4 there (line 15)   = _____
5 they (line 20)   = _____

WRITING

11 Read this letter. The style isn't very good. Write it again and replace the underlined words with pronouns.

142 Amazonas
Quito
3. 4. 95

Dear Jean,

I love Quito, (1) <u>Quito</u> is wonderful. (2) <u>Quito</u> has new and old buildings which makes (3) <u>Quito</u> very interesting.
The people are really friendly. (4) <u>The people</u> always try to help tourists. I have two lovely new Ecuadorian friends. I met (5) <u>two lovely new Ecuadorian friends</u> on the first day I arrived. (6) <u>The two lovely new Ecuadorian friends</u> take me to beautiful new places every night.
The weather is beautiful, too. (7) <u>The weather</u> isn't too hot and (8) <u>the weather</u> is never cold. I want to stay in Quito forever. (9) <u>Quito</u> is like home to me, but sadly I have to leave next week.

See you soon.
Love

Josephine

DICTATION

Pronunciation

12 [5.3]   Listen and complete B's sentences with the words in the box. They all have the same pronunciation /ðeə/.

┌─────────────────────────┐
│ they're   their   there │
└─────────────────────────┘

1 A: Freda and Max are here.

   B: _____

2 A: Where are my shoes?

   B: _____

3 A: I can't find Mr and Mrs Hudson's house.

   B: _____

4 A: Stephanie and James both have expensive cars.

   B: _____

142 Amazonas
Quito
3. 4. 95

Dear Jean,

Love

Josephine

Daily bread

GRAMMAR

Countable and uncountable nouns

1 Put the words in the box in the correct place in the table. Write the singular **and** plural form for the countable nouns.

> cat water journey apple sugar cream
> luggage furniture milk potato salt pen
> newspaper bottle shampoo toothpaste
> toothbrush money stamp food

Countable nouns	Uncountable nouns
cat/cats	*water*

2 Complete the sentences with *a* or *an*, *some* or *any*. Sometimes there is more than one possibility.

1 Can I have <u>*an*</u> apple, please?

2 I need _____ water. I'm thirsty.

3 Did you buy _____ newspapers today?

4 I'd like _____ cream in my coffee, please.

5 Do you want _____ tea?

6 I've got _____ terrible headache.

7 Have you got _____ luggage with you?

8 There's _____ more luggage in the car.

9 I need _____ new furniture for this room.

10 I haven't got _____ pen.

11 Just a moment. I'll get _____ paper and write this down.

Much/many/a lot (of)/a few/a little

3 Which sentence is correct?

1 a) *How many potatoes do you want?* ✓
   b) How much potatoes do you want? ✗

2 a) I haven't got many money. __
   b) I haven't got much money. __

3 a) I'm sorry I can't give you any paper. I haven't got much. __
   b) I'm sorry I can't give you any paper. I haven't got a lot of. __

4 a) I bought a few CDs today. __
   b) I bought a little CDs today. __

5 a) Not too many water, please. Just a few. __
   b) Not too much water, please. Just a little. __

6 a) Jane reads much books. __
   b) Jane reads a lot of books. __

7 a) They didn't give me many informations about the course. __
   b) They didn't give me much information about the course. __

8 a) I only put a little salt on the potatoes. __
   b) I only put a few salts on the potatoes. __

4 a) Complete this story with the words in the box. Sometimes there is more than one possibility.

some   any   much   many   few   little

Once upon a time there was a little girl called Little Red Riding Hood. Her Grandmother lived in the forest a (1) _few_ kilometres from Red Riding Hood's village. The Grandmother was ill and she didn't have (2) _____ food to eat so Red put (3) _____ food into a basket to take to her. When Red was walking through the forest, she met a wolf.

'What have you got in your basket?' the Wolf asked.

'I'm sorry, Wolf,' said Red, 'but I haven't got (4) _____ time to talk. My Grandmother's ill and I'm taking (5) _____ food to her.'

'Oh, food. I'm very interested in food,' said the Wolf. 'What kind of food?'

'Not a lot. A (6) _____ apples, (7) _____ bread, (8) _____ wine, a (9) _____ cheese, a (10) _____ potatoes, a (11) _____ cakes, (12) _____ tea and a (13) _____ sugar,' Red said.

'So you haven't got (14) _____ meat?' asked the Wolf.

'No, I haven't.' said Red.

'And you haven't got (15) _____ vegetables, only potatoes,' continued the Wolf.

'Yes. Only a (16) _____ potatoes,' answered Red.

'Well!' said the Wolf. 'That's a terrible diet! I'm not surprised your Grandmother's ill.'

'But she's a vegetarian!' said Red, angrily.

'Well, she needs a (17) _____ eggs,' replied the Wolf.

'Don't you read (18) _____ newspapers?' asked Red. 'There was an article in *The Sun* yesterday. It says eggs are bad for us.'

'Rubbish!' shouted the Wolf.

Their discussion went on through the night and into the next day. Sadly, Red's Grandmother, who was a hundred years old, became very weak and died waiting for the food!

b) [📼 6.1]   Listen and check your answers.

VOCABULARY

Food

5 Complete these words with the missing vowels.

1 f _ s h
2 m _ _ t
3 b _ n _ n _
4 _ p p l _
5 _ r _ n g _
6 s t r _ w b _ r r _ _ s
7 c _ _ l _ f l _ w _ r
8 y _ g h _ r t
9 c h _ _ s _
10 p _ t _ t _
11 c h _ c k _ n
12 l _ m b
13 p _ s t _

6 Match the words with the picture. Use a dictionary to help you.

1 napkin ___	9 glass ___
2 dessert	10 teaspoon ___
spoon ___	11 candle ___
3 knife ___	12 salt and
4 fork ___	pepper
5 plate ___	pots ___
6 cup ___	13 bowl ___
7 mug ___	14 side
8 saucer ___	plate ___

LISTENING

Sylvia

Sophie

When young people leave home, do they eat enough good food?

7 a) Look at the photographs of Sophie, Sylvia and David. Who do you think has a good diet?

b) [🔲 6.2]   Listen to Sophie, Sylvia and David. Check your answer.

c) Listen again. Write *True* (T) or *False* (F) next to these sentences.

SOPHIE DREW

1 Sophie thinks she should eat fruit and vegetables every day. __F__

2 Sophie's mother thinks Sophie has a bad diet. ____

3 Sophie likes going home at weekends. ____

4 Sophie is often ill. ____

SYLVIA STAPLETON

5 Sylvia doesn't eat much before her evening meal. ____

6 Sylvia is thin. ____

7 Sylvia isn't a vegetarian. ____

8 Sylvia wears big sweaters to look fatter. ____

DAVID CONROY

9 David likes cooking different meals. ____

10 He always has two big meals a day. ____

11 He only had a sandwich for his meal last night. ____

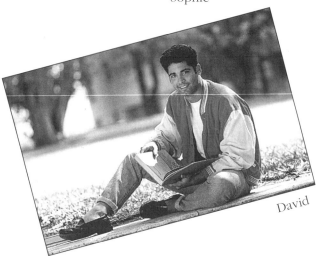

David

PRONUNCIATION

Sound and spelling /ɔ:/

8 [🔲 6.3]   Listen and complete the missing letters in these words. All the words have the sound /ɔ:/.

1 w/ɔ:/k _____
2 d/ɔ:/ _____
3 f/ɔ:/teen _____
4 s/ɔ:/ _____

9 a) Circle the words which have the sound /ɔ:/.

(horse) water wood thought want won't your short tall pool took floor morning hour

b) [🔲 6.4]   Listen and check your answers.

DICTATION

Contractions and weak forms

10 [📼 6.5] You are going to hear Amy read a letter from her Spanish friend, Juan. Listen and complete the sentences.

Barcelona

28 May

Dear Amy,

(1) _I've_ got (2) _____ good news. (3) _____ coming to England in (4) _____ middle (5) _____ June (6) _____ make (7) _____ film (8) _____ (9) _____ travel agent here in Spain. Do you think I could stay with you (10) _____ two (11) _____ three nights until I (12) _____ find (13) _____ nice cheap hotel? (14) _____ cook and (15) _____ buy the wine!

    Sorry this letter is so short, but I'm really busy at the moment. Please let (16) _____ know (17) _____ soon (18) _____ possible if I can stay with you.

    Looking forward to hearing from you.

    Love Juan

PS My plane arrives (19) _____ ten in the morning on 16 June.

WRITING

Putting information in the correct order

11 Read Amy's letter to Juan and look at the map. Then write these directions in the middle paragraph. Use the words in the box to put the information in the correct order.

Next   Finally   After that   First   Then

a) You get a train to Kingsbridge Station.
b) You catch a number 22 bus to Pitney, and get off at the High Street.
c) You cross over the road.
d) You walk up the hill.
e) You turn right into Bleaker Street.

---

11 Bleaker St

Pitney

31 May

Dear Juan,

Thank you for your letter which arrived this morning. It was great to hear you're coming over to England – of course you can stay at my place.

    As you know I live in Pitney now, in quite a big house. So you don't need to go to a hotel, you can just stay here. I'll give you directions and I'll leave the front door key under a milk bottle on the step. I usually get home from work about 7 pm, so get cooking!

    Here are the directions.

Number 11 is the fourth house on the left. See you on 16 June.

Love Amy

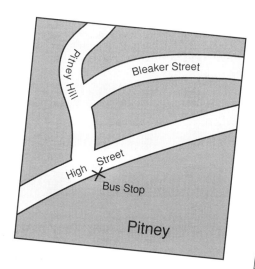

How do you feel about ...?

GRAMMAR

Past Simple and past participles

1 Complete this table with the correct form of the verb. They are all irregular verbs.

Base Form	Past Simple	Past Participle
come	_came_	_come_
_____	_____	gone
_____	_____	told
see	_____	_____
_____	bought	_____
_____	_____	given
take	_____	_____
_____	sent	_____
_____	_____	drunk
eat	_____	_____
_____	had	_____
_____	_____	thought

Present Perfect or Past Simple?

2 Write questions for these answers. Use the Present Perfect or the Past Simple. Use the words in brackets to help you.

1 (ever/eat/Thai food)

A: _Have you ever eaten Thai food?_

B: No, I haven't. Is it nice?

2 (see/the film/last night)

A: _Did you see the film last night?_

B: Yes, I did. It was great.

3 (ever/be/Argentina)

A: _____

B: Yes, I have. I went to Buenos Aires in 1992.

4 (be/ill/last week)

A: _____

B: Yes, I was. I had flu.

5 (finish/report/yet)

A: _____

B: No, I haven't. I'm going to finish it tonight.

6 (see/John)

A: _____

B: Yes, I have. He's just gone into Sue's office.

7 (go/Dan's party on Saturday)

A: _____

B: No, I didn't. I was ill.

8 (see/Keanu Reeves' new film)

A: _____

B: No, I haven't. Is it good?

Been or *gone*?

She's been to France. = She went to France and she has returned.

She's gone to France = She is in France now. She hasn't returned yet.

3 Circle the correct past participle.

1 A: Can I speak to Peter please?

B: He's not here. He's *been*/*gone* to work.

2 You look very well. Have you *been*/*gone* on holiday?

3 I can't find Jacob anywhere. Do you know where he's *been*/*gone*?

4 I put my pen on that desk. Where's it *been*/*gone*?

5 Barbara's *been*/*gone* to Brazil. She came back last week.

6 A: Is there any milk?

B: No, but Martha's *been*/*gone* to the shop. She'll be back soon.

Present Perfect: negatives

4 Use the words in brackets to make negative sentences.

1 Brian's been to India.
   (*China*) *But he hasn't been to China.*

2 We've read that newspaper.
   (*this one*) _____.

3 Hilary's hurt her arm.
   (*broken it*) _____.

4 I've driven a Porsche.
   (*Mercedes*) _____.

5 They've bought some wine.
   (*beer*) _____.

6 I've told Kevin about the party.
   (*Ben*) _____.

Present Perfect or Past Simple?

5 Paul and Linda are talking about their friend Susan.

a) Circle the correct form of the verb.

1 PAUL: *Has Susan told/Did Susan tell* you her good news yet?

   LINDA: No. What is it?

2 PAUL: *She's passed/She passed* her driving test yesterday.

   LINDA: Oh, great news.

3 PAUL: *Her mother's just bought/Her mother just bought* her a car.

   LINDA: What is it?

4 PAUL: It's a small Italian car, but she *hasn't told/didn't tell* Susan yet. It's a surprise for her birthday.

5 LINDA: *Did you buy/Have you bought* her a present yet?

   PAUL: No, but I could buy her some petrol!

b) [📼 7.1]   Listen and check your answers.

VOCABULARY

Adjectives and prepositions

6 Complete the sentences with one of the prepositions in the box.

about	of	with	in

1 Henry was worried __*about*__ his exam.
2 I'm not frightened _____ spiders.
3 I'm really angry _____ you!
4 I'm bored _____ this weather!
5 I'm very excited _____ winning that money.
6 John's very depressed _____ his exam results.
7 I'm not very interested _____ murder stories.
8 I'm really annoyed _____ you. You're always late!
9 Green vegetables are very good _____ you.

READING

Finishing relationships

7 Ben, a computer sales assistant, and Nina, a student, talk about finishing relationships. They are both twenty-one.

a) Think about these questions before you read the articles.

1 Do you think it is easy to finish a relationship?
2 Have you ever finished a relationship with a boyfriend or girlfriend? How did you feel?
3 Has a boyfriend or girlfriend ever finished with you? How did you feel?

b) Read the articles. Which of these ways of finishing do they **not** talk about?

1 Have a few drinks and tell the person it's finished.
2 Tell the person but try to be nice.
3 Write a letter telling the person it's finished.
4 Ask a friend to tell the person it's finished.

c) Write *True* (T) or *False* (F) next to these sentences.

1 Ben usually tells the girl he wants to end the relationship. _T_

2 Nina always tells the boy she wants to finish the relationship._____

3 Ben likes to be friends with the girl after the relationship has finished._____

4 Ben's last girlfriend got very angry when he finished with her._____

5 When Nina doesn't want to talk to a boy on the phone, her friends tell the boy she's not at home._____

'I don't have ONE way of finishing with a girlfriend, but I always try to be nice. I like it when we are still friends because I don't like bad feelings. Sometimes I get into difficult situations. Once I met a girl at a party but the next day when I saw her I didn't like her. I had to tell her that I didn't want to meet her again. She was really angry. That wasn't very good, but I think you have to tell the truth.
It was different with my last girlfriend. When I told her I wanted to end the relationship, we sat down and talked about why I wanted to finish. That was a better way.'

Ben

'I have lots of ways of finishing with boyfriends. Sometimes I hide from them, and sometimes I have a few glasses of wine then tell them I want to finish the relationship.
Sometimes my friends help me. When the boy phones, my friends tell him I'm out and that I'll phone him later, but I don't. Once my friend started a relationship with a boy I wanted to finish with. That was great because I didn't have to do anything.'

Nina

WRITING

FOUND DEAD

8 a) Complete the story with *a* or *the*.

Yesterday Megan went on (1) __*a*__ train to London to see (2) _____ friend. She caught (3) _____ nine o'clock train from Oxford to London. She sat next to (4) _____ man who was wearing (5) _____ brown coat. (6) _____ man began to talk to her and said, 'Excuse me. I've never been to London before. Is there (7) _____ good hotel near Hyde Park?'

Megan said, '(8) _____ Hilton is (9) _____ good hotel, but it's very expensive.'

(10) _____ man said, 'Thank you.' After that he didn't talk to Megan. (11) _____ next day Megan bought (12) _____ newspaper. On (13) _____ front page there was (14) _____ photograph of (15) _____ same man. He was dead.

b) [📼 7.2] Listen and check your answers.

9 Finish the story. Use these questions to help you.

- Who was the man?
- Who killed him?
- Why did they kill him?
- Did the police catch the people who killed him?

The man's name was … _____

_____

_____

_____

_____

_____

_____

_____

_____

_____

DICTATION

Questions and pronunciation

10 a) [📼 7.3]   Listen and complete the sentences.

1 __*Have*__ you __*seen*__ my __*keys*__?
2 _____ _____ you _____ those _____?
3 _____ Peter _____ to _____ _____?
4 _____ you _____ the _____?
5 _____ you _____ yesterday?
6 _____ David _____ on Monday?

b) Listen again. Mark the word which has the most stress in each question.

All work and no play

GRAMMAR

To or -ing?

1 Which of these verbs are followed by *to*? Which verbs are followed by *-ing*? Put the verbs in the correct place.

> decide want hope
> enjoy promise manage
> expect finish offer miss
> forget would like like

To + Base form
decide to do

Base form + -ing
enjoy doing

2 a) Complete this story with the correct form of the verbs in brackets. Sometimes *to* and *-ing* are possible.

In 1990 my doctor said I was working too hard and I had to have a holiday. I managed (*get*) (1) _to get_ two weeks' holiday from work. I wanted (*go*) (2) _____ to Greece and learn (*dive*) (3)_____. I like (*be*) (4)_____ near the sea and I love (*swim*) (5)_____ in it. I have a friend who works in a travel agent's and she offered (*arrange*) (6) _____ the holiday for me. She promised (*find*) (7)_____ me a cheap hotel to stay in. All the plans were ready.

I'm frightened of (*fly*) (8)_____ so I decided (*drive*) (9) _____ across Europe to Greece. It was exciting (*travel*) (10)_____ through all the different countries. However, when I arrived in Greece I was disappointed (*find*) (11) _____ the hotel was not near the sea, but in a town about thirty kilometres inland. The diving school was good but I didn't enjoy (*be*) (12)_____ frightened all the time. On the third day I was too frightened to go down under water and I had terrible pains in my stomach. A doctor came to see me and said, 'You need to rest. Your problem is stress.' So I came home and went back to work. I was happy (*sit*) (13) _____ in front of my computer again!

b) [8.1] Listen and check your answers.

Adjectives and adjectives + prepositions

3 Complete these sentences with the *to* or *-ing* form of the verbs in brackets. Sometimes *to* and *-ing* are possible.

1 I was sad (hear) _to hear_ you failed your driving test.
2 I'm frightened of (swim) _____ in the sea.
3 John's interested in (buy) _____ your bicycle.
4 I'm happy (sleep) _____ on the floor if there isn't a bed.
5 I'm thinking about (go) _____ to Switzerland for a holiday.
6 Sarah's worried about (go) _____ to the dentist's.
7 It's interesting (watch) _____ young children playing games.

4 Circle the preposition which goes with these verbs and adjectives.

1 I'm thinking *to/about* buying a motorbike.
2 Mike's bored *with/about* his job.
3 Samantha's good *at/in* working with computers.
4 I'm angry *to/with* Jack. He broke my TV.
5 I'm angry *about/to* this room. It's so untidy!
6 The policeman stopped us *to/from* leaving the building.
7 Don't forget to thank Sue *for/about* the present.
8 Gillie won't know the answer. She's really bad *with/at* mathematics.
9 It's very nice *about/of* you to help me carry these bags.
10 Be quiet! I'm fed up *with/for* all the noise!

VOCABULARY

Jobs

5 a) Match the jobs with the pictures.

1 engi'**neer** _C_
2 jeweller _____
3 gardener _____
4 cook or chef _____
5 librarian _____
6 architect _____
7 dentist _____
8 decorator _____
9 scientist _____
10 lawyer _____
11 plumber _____
12 carpenter _____
13 electrician _____
14 secretary _____

b) [8.2] Listen and mark the stressed syllable in each word.

6 Complete the sentences with the correct form of one of the verbs in the box. Use the verbs only once.

design   take   post   type   decorate   make
build   plant

1 They're going to _ *build* _ a bridge over that road.
2 Excuse me. Can you _____ a photograph of me and my friend?
3 When you go out, can you _____ this letter for me, please?
4 I must _____ some vegetables this year.
5 My secretary _____ two letters for me, but I can't find them.
6 These walls look terrible. We must _____ this room soon.
7 Who _____ this house? It's beautiful.
8 I'm going to ask Jane to _____ me a coffee table. She's a very good carpenter.

A    B

C    D    E    F

G    H    I    J

K    L   M   N

31

LISTENING

You're going to listen to
a junior doctor talking about her work.

7 a) Before you listen, which information
do you think is correct? Tick (✓) a) or b).

1 Many junior doctors work
   a) more than 83 hours a week. ___
   b) 50 hours a week. ___

2 When the junior doctor works
overtime (extra hours)
   a) she gets a lot of money. ___
   b) she gets very little money. ___

3 Junior doctors are
   a) always polite to patients. ___
   b) sometimes impolite to
      patients. ___

b) [📼 8.3]   Now listen to Mandy Robinson
and check your answers.

8 What do these words and expressions mean?
Use a dictionary to help you.

1 to work long hours
   a) to work in the night   **✗**
   b) to work a lot of hours every day   **✓**
2 a bleeper
   a) a small machine which doctors
     carry like a telephone   ___
   b) an alarm clock   ___
3 to earn money
   a) money you get for working   ___
   b) to save money in a bank   ___
4 I'm asleep
   a) sleeping   ___
   b) not sleeping   ___
5 annoyed
   a) tired   ___
   b) angry   ___

9 Listen again and answer these questions.

1 Is this Mandy's first job in a hospital?
   Yes, it is.

2 What is the rule about how many hours a junior
doctor should work in a week?

3 How many calls did Mandy get on the first
weekend she worked in the hospital?

4 Does Mandy have to carry her bleeper with her
all the time?

5 Do junior doctors earn a lot of money?

6 What is Mandy frightened of doing?

7 Why is she impolite sometimes?

8 Is she married?

PRONUNCIATION

Sound and spelling: *o*

10 a) [📼 8.4]   Listen to four different ways we
can pronounce the letter *o*.

/əʊ/	/aʊ/	/ʌ/	/ɒ/
n<u>o</u>	c<u>ow</u>	s<u>o</u>n	g<u>o</u>t

b) [📼 8.5]   Now listen to the words in the
box and write them in the correct place.

now   broken   come   throw   clock   lost   so sock   don't   know   flower   money   lovely snow   go

DICTATION

Names, dates, numbers and countries

11 [📼 8.6] Listen and complete the job application form.

Surname (1) _____
First name(s) (2) _____
Mr/Mrs/Miss/Mrs (3) _____
Nationality (5) _____ Age (4) _____
Address 16 (6) _____
(7) _____
Tel No (8) _____ St,
_____ W1

Previous experience as a waiter/waitress
McDonald's in (9) _____
Pasta Palace in (10) _____ 1993–1995
The Savoy in (12) _____ (11) _____ –1993
_____ 1990 – (13)

WRITING

A formal letter

12 Tim has to write a letter to send with his application form. Write this information in the correct places in the letter.

1 Dear Madam
2 24 April
3 Yours faithfully
4  *Timothy Brawnly*

5 16 Green St
London W1
6 The Manageress
Angelo's Restaurant
212 Piccadilly
London W1
7 I look forward to hearing from you.
8 I have just returned from Moscow and as I am not working at the moment I could come for an interview any day during the week.
9 Please find enclosed my application for the position of Head Waiter at Angelo's restaurant. I am also sending references from the managers of the Pasta Palace and The Savoy.

a)

h)

i)

b) Dear Madam

c)

d)

e)

f)

g)

A place of your own

GRAMMAR

Might, will and *won't*

1 a) Complete these conversations with *might, will* or *won't*.

1 BRUCE: What's the matter?

   SUE: My German and Spanish exams are today. I know I (*fail*) (1) _'ll fail_ .

   BRUCE: I'm sure you (*not fail*) (2) _____. You're really good at languages.

   SUE: Well, I (*pass*) (3) _____ Spanish if I'm lucky, but I definitely (*not pass*)

      (4) _____ German. I haven't done any work on German for weeks.

2 SARAH: Why are you taking a raincoat?

   BEN: It (*rain*) (1) _____ later. You never know.

   SARAH: It's sunny and there are no clouds. It (*not rain*) (2) _____.

   BEN: Maybe not. I expect Mum (*take*) (3) _____ her umbrella so I (*leave*) (4)

      _____ my raincoat here.

3 AMY: Can you help me tidy this room, please? Mum (*be*) (1) _____ really angry with us.

   LUCY: What time's she coming home?

   AMY: She finishes work at six o'clock. She (*be*) (2) _____ back in a few minutes.

4 DAN: Are you doing anything tonight, Jane?

   JANE: I'm not sure. I (*go*) (1) _____ to see Mary. I haven't seen her this week. Why?

   DAN: I'm going to see *Frankenstein*. I mean the film *Frankenstein*. Mary can come, too.

   JANE: No, Mary (*not want*) (2) _____ to see that. She hates horror films.

b) [🔊 9.1] Listen and check your answers.

First Conditional

2 Match words from A and B to make sentences.

A	**B**
1 If it's sunny tomorrow,	a) we'll miss the plane.
2 If you want something to eat,	b) I'll buy a bottle for you.
3 If you like stories,	c) I'll go to the beach.
4 If we don't leave now,	d) will you buy me a newspaper?
5 If you want some wine with dinner,	e) you'll pass your exams.
6 If you study a lot,	f) you'll love this book.
7 If you go to the shop,	g) I'll cook a pizza.

First Conditional and *might*

3 Carol is going to Paris to study art. Her mother is very worried.

a) What does Carol say to her mother? Write sentences with *if*.

1 MOTHER: You might lose your passport!

   CAROL: *If I lose my passport, I'll go to the embassy.* (go to the embassy)

2 MOTHER: You might not find a flat.

   CAROL: *If I don't find a flat, I'll stay with Françoise.* (stay with Françoise)

3 MOTHER: You might get ill!

   CAROL: If _____
   (*find a doctor*)

4 MOTHER: You might not have enough money!

   CAROL: If _____
   (*get a job*)

5 MOTHER: You might not find a job!

   CAROL: If _____
   (*ask you for more money*)

6 MOTHER: You might not like Paris.

   CAROL: If _____
   (*come home*)

7 MOTHER: You might find a boyfriend and get married!

   CAROL: If _____
   (*invite you to the wedding*)

   MOTHER: Oh, thank you dear. I haven't got anything to worry about then!

b) [🖭 9.2]   Listen and check your answers.

First Conditional: negative sentences

4 Complete these sentences with the correct form of the verbs in brackets.

1 If he (*not come*) _doesn't come_ , I (*not stay*) _won't stay_ .

2 If I (*buy*) _____ that jacket, I (*not have*) _____ enough money for some trousers.

3 If you (*not want*) _____ stay at the party, I (*take*) _____ you home.

4 If you (*be*) _____ late, I (*not wait*) _____ for you.

5 If you (*not have got*) _____ time to write to me, (*you phone*) _____ me?

6 If he (*not like*) _____ wine, I (*buy*) _____ some beer.

7 If we (*not leave*) _____, we (*not catch*) _____ the train.

8 If it rains, I (*not play*) _____ tennis.

VOCABULARY

5 Things in the house. The things in each circle are similar but different. Match the words with the pictures.

1 dressing table _____
2 chair _____
3 bookshelf _____
4 carpet _____
5 plug _____
6 cup _____
7 curtains _____
8 rug _____
9 switch _____
10 mug _____
11 blinds _____
12 shutters _____
13 armchair _____
14 bookcase _____
15 glass _____
16 stool _____
17 table _____

PRONUNCIATION

Word stress

6 a) [🔊 9.3] Listen to the words in Vocabulary. Mark the stressed syllable in each word.

b) Look at the words with more than one syllable. Do we stress the first or the second syllable in these words?

LISTENING

Home sweet home!

7 Make a list of:

Good things about **not** living in the city	Good things about living in the city
It's quiet.	

8 Linda and Graham are talking about where they live.

a) [🔊 9.4] Listen. Do they talk about any of the things on your lists?

b) Listen again. What do Linda and Graham talk about? Match the pictures with the people. Two of the pictures go with Linda **and** Graham.

LINDA _____ *B* _____
GRAHAM _____

36

c) Listen to Linda again and answer these questions.

1 Why didn't Linda like living in the city?

_____

_____

2 What are the problems with Linda's house?

_____

_____

3 What does she do when she's frightened?

_____

4 What is Linda's job?

_____

d) Listen to Graham again and answer these questions.

1 Where does Graham work?

_____

2 Why did he buy a flat near the city centre?

_____

3 Why can't he buy a house with a garden?

_____

4 Why does he want a garden?

_____

WRITING

Telling a story

10 a) Complete the story with words from the box where you see a number. Ignore the ▲ for the moment.

> lake   afternoon   swam   sat   two   park
> danger   can   arm

Joanna was walking through the (1) _park_ yesterday (2) _____ when she heard someone scream. The noise came from the lake so she ran as ▲_____ as she could and got to the lake very ▲_____ . She saw (3) _____ boys. The older boy was in the lake and the other one was standing by the side of the lake. Joanna ▲_____ took off her jacket, jumped into the (4) _____ and swam to the boy in the water. When she got to him, he began to shout at her.

Joanna turned the boy ▲_____ on to his back and (5) _____ with him to where the younger boy was standing. She pulled the older boy out of the water and (6) _____ down.

'What are you doing?' asked the younger boy.

'I've just saved your friend's life,' said Joanna.

'But I wasn't in (7) _____, I (8) _____ swim!' said the older boy.

'Why did you scream so ▲_____ ?' asked Joanna.

'I didn't!' said the boy.

'I screamed,' said the younger boy. 'There was a bee on my (9) _____.'

b) Complete the story with the adverbs in the box where you see ▲.

> fast   immediately   quickly   loudly   carefully

c) [📼 9.5]   Listen and check your answers.

DICTATION

Contracted forms

11 [📼 9.6]   Listen and complete these sentences.

1 _____, we'll be late.

2 If we're late, _____.

3 If we don't catch the plane, _____.

4 If I don't have a holiday, _____!

5 Look, if you stop talking, _____!

Britain and the British

GRAMMAR:
Revision of Units 1–10

1 Correct the underlined mistakes.

1 He <u>don't</u> know the answer. (Unit 1)
   He doesn't know the answer.

2 When <u>you're coming</u> to England? (Unit 2)
   _____

3 <u>Do</u> he work in a bank? (Unit 2)
   _____

4 <u>Do</u> you go to work yesterday? (Unit 3)
   _____

5 Yesterday I <u>have been</u> to the dentist. (Unit 3)
   _____

6 When Lorna arrived <u>I'm eating</u> my dinner. (Unit 3)
   _____

7 I usually wear a skirt, but today I <u>wear</u> jeans. (Unit 5)
   _____

8 I like that bag. I think I <u>buy</u> it. (Unit 5)
   _____

9 <u>Have</u> John left yet? (Unit 7)
   _____

10 Jack would like <u>buying</u> my old car. (Unit 8)
   _____

11 Mary enjoys <u>to watch</u> films. (Unit 8)
   _____

12 I finished <u>read</u> that book. (Unit 8)
   _____

13 <u>I'll</u> come tonight, but I'm not sure. (Unit 9)
   _____

14 If <u>I'll</u> go to the shop, I'll buy you a newspaper. (Unit 9)
   _____

2 Write questions for these sentences.

1 Rosie can come to dinner on Friday.
   Can Rosie come to dinner on Friday?

2 Michelle works at the university.
   Where _____ ?

3 You have to get up at 8 am tomorrow.
   What time _____ ?

4 Sam's got three sisters.
   How many _____ ?

5 Gill bought a new bike last week.
   What _____ ?

6 If Janice comes to London, she'll stay at the Park Hotel.
   Where _____ ?

7 Simon lives in that house.
   Who _____ ?

8 Stephen lives in Berlin.
   Where _____ ?

Questions and short answers

3 Match a question from A with a short answer from B.

A	B
1 Was John playing tennis when you saw him?	a) Yes, she will.
2 Who wants fish?	b) Yes, she is.
3 Has Thomas left for Brazil yet?	c) No, he isn't.
4 Have you seen the film *Mask 3* yet?	d) No, I don't.
5 If Corinne comes to the wedding, will she stay at your house?	e) No, he didn't.
6 Do you play tennis very often?	f) No, I haven't.
7 Is Jane coming on Monday?	g) Yes, he has.
8 Did John get the answer right?	h) Rosie does.
9 Is Bill ill?	i) Yes, he was.

Word order: position of adverbs

4 Put the words in the correct order to make sentences.

1 never/seen/film/horror/she/a/has
She has never seen a horror film.

2 go/usually/I/cinema/Friday/on/to/the

_____.

3 have/read/book/I/just/this

_____.

4 work/he/sometimes/early/leaves

_____.

5 yet/I/finished/not/have/homework/my

_____.

VOCABULARY

5 Divide the words in the box into four groups. Write each word in the correct place. Use a dictionary to help you.

belt trainers neck gloves wrist blinds pilot fingers toes mug engineer stool zip socks politician rug shoulder glass plug bra armchair mechanic sink dishwasher

In the house	Jobs
blinds	
Things you wear	**Parts of the body**

READING

Are you old enough?

6 a) Read the article. What are the differences and similarities between British law and the law in your country?

ARE YOU OLD ENOUGH?

You can drink alcohol in Britain, but you can't buy alcohol from a shop or a pub before you are **eighteen**. Some pub landladies and landlords allow parents to bring children into pubs in the daytime, but they still have to be **eighteen** before they can drink any alcohol.

You can get married at the age of **sixteen** if your parents agree to the marriage. If they don't agree, then you have to wait until you're **eighteen**. However, in Scotland, you can get married at **sixteen** without your parents' permission.

You can have a part-time job when you're **thirteen** years old, but the job mustn't be in school hours. Some **thirteen**-year-olds deliver newspapers to people's homes before they go to school. Babysitting is a very common part-time job, especially for teenage girls, but you can't do this until you're **fourteen**. You can't get a full-time job until you are **sixteen**, which is the age when you are allowed to leave school if you don't want to go to university. You also have to be **sixteen** to buy cigarettes.

When you are **seventeen** you are allowed to ride a motorbike or drive a car, but you can ride a moped when you are **sixteen**. A moped is like a motorbike but it has a very small engine.

Eighteen is an important age. When you are **eighteen** you can marry, you can own land and buildings, you can drink in pubs, and in Britain you can get a tattoo.

b) Look at the pictures. How old do you have to be to do these things in Britain? Write the age next to each picture.

A   B   C   *18*

D   E   F

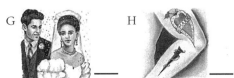

G   H

WRITING

7 You have just returned to your country after six months in England. You went there to learn English. You stayed with an English family, Jean and Jeff Staple and their two children, Alice and Sam. You realise you have left your English book in the cupboard in your room at Mr and Mrs Staples' house. You need the book because you made a lot of useful notes in it.

Write a letter to the Staples. Follow the instructions in brackets and complete the sentences.

(your address) _____

_____

(date) _____

Dear Jean, Jeff and family,

I arrived home (say when) <u>on Friday</u>, (and/but) _____ the journey was (describe the journey) _____. It's (describe how it feels) _____ to be back with my (say who) _____, but I miss (say what/who) _____. I want to thank you again for the (adjective) _____ time I had with you. You are a (adjective) _____ family.

When I unpacked my bags I couldn't find my English book. (say where/left) _____ It's really important because (give reasons) _____. Could (polite request) _____. I hope this isn't too much trouble for you. I'll send a money order to pay for the postage.

I'm going to rest for (how long) _____ and then I (what are your plans) _____ _____.

Please write if you have time. I would love to have news about you all.
(Love/Best wishes) _____
(your name) _____

DICTATION

Sound and spelling: *c*

8 [🔲 10.1] Listen and complete these sentences.

1 The _____ left a _____ of _____ on the _____.
2 _____ you go to the _____ for me, and get my _____?
3 I _____ _____ what to have for _____.
4 I bought a _____ _____ for tonight. It looks _____.
5 I'm _____ she's a _____.
6 There's been a terrible _____ _____.

9 a) [🔲 10.2] Listen to five different ways we can pronounce the letter *c*.

/ k /	/ s /	/ tʃ /	/ ʃ /	/ ks /
<u>c</u>at	pie<u>c</u>e	<u>c</u>hair	spe<u>c</u>ial	ac<u>c</u>ept

b) [🔲 10.3] Listen to the words and complete the table.

Key

Unit 1

GRAMMAR

Questions and answers

2
Jeremy: A, D
Jean-Paul: B, C

3
1   When do Jayne and Jeremy wake up?
2   Who is Imogen?
3   What does Jeremy have for breakfast?
4   What does Jeremy do at the weekend?
5   What does Jean-Paul Gaultier do?
6   How does Jean-Paul get to work?
7   Where is Jean-Paul's flat?
8   When does Jean-Paul go to bed?

Subject and object questions

4
1   What (films) does Mary like?
    Who likes horror films?

2   Who drives an Italian car?
    What (car) does Jan drive?

3   What does Simon have for breakfast?
    Who has toast and coffee for breakfast?

Questions with *whose*

5
3   A: Whose pen is this?   B: It's Gordon's.
4   A: Whose is this bag?   B: It's Julia's.
5   A: Whose books are these?   B: They're Pat's.
6   A: Whose are these flowers?   B: They're Susan's.
7   A: Whose are these glasses?   B: They're Jane's.
8   A: Whose hat is this?   B: It's Dan's.

VOCABULARY AND PRONUNCIATION

Nationalities and countries: word stress

6a)
2   D   9   E
3   D   10 A
4   C   11 A
5   6   12 B
6   D   13 6
7   A   14 B
8   B   15 B

7a)
2   'Germany
3   'Egypt
4   'Scotland
5   'Italy
6   Bra'zil
7   'Hungary

8
3   Italian   6   German
4   correct   7   Scotland
5   Africa   8   correct

LISTENING

9
WESTMINSTER UNIVERSITY
STUDENT INFORMATION

First name   Sue
Surname   Burnet
Course   Business Studies
Room   2F
Starting Date   10 October
Time   9.30 am
Why did you choose this course?
I want to have my own company, buying and selling
motorbikes.

WRITING

Punctuation

10
1   Peter starts his new job on 1 May.
2   Julia travels to France, Brazil, America and Spain every
    year.
3   Your plane leaves on Monday at 18.00 hours and you
    arrive in Madrid at 20.00 hours.
4   I want to leave about 7.45 tomorrow morning. Can you
    wake me up at 6 o'clock?
5   My next dentist's appointment is at 2.15 pm on Tuesday
    30 September.
6   When is Amybeth's birthday? It's on 21 December.

DICTATION

Dates and times

11
2   Julia travels to Italy, Peru, America and Germany every
    year.
3   Your plane leaves on Sunday at eighteen thirty hours, and
    you arrive in London at twenty one hundred hours.
4   I want to leave about seven thirty tomorrow morning.
    Can you wake me up at a quarter to six?
5   My next dentist's appointment is at two forty five on
    Wednesday the twenty ninth November.
6   When is Amybeth's birthday? It's on the first of
    December.

Unit 2

GRAMMAR

Present Continuous or Present Simple

1
2   He's *smiling* and he's happy.
    He always *shouts* at everyone on Mondays!

3 Look, he's *having* lunch in the office cafeteria!
He *doesn't eat* here very often, does he?
He usually *goes* out for lunch.
4 It's after 5 o'clock and he's *working*!
But he never *works* this late!
5 Who *is Simon talking* to?
He always *falls* in love with new women in the office.

Short answers

2
3 No, he doesn't.
4 No, he doesn't.
5 Yes, he is.
6 Yes, he does.
7 No, he isn't.

Question forms

3a)
2 Where are Sam and Jane living now?
3 Do you sell stamps?
4 Do they always drink wine with their meals?
5 When does the bank close?
6 Does Pamela often play tennis at the weekends?
7 Who is making that noise?

b)
b – 6   e – 5
c – 2   f – 4
d – 7   g – 1

Frequency adverbs

4
2 Janet *always plays* tennis on Mondays.
3 Janet *rarely plays* tennis on Tuesdays.
4 Janet *usually plays* tennis on Wednesdays.
5 Janet *never plays* tennis on Thursdays but she always goes swimming.
6 Janet *sometimes plays* tennis on Fridays.
7 Janet *often plays* tennis on Saturdays.
8 Janet *never plays* tennis on Sundays but she *always goes* swimming.

VOCABULARY

5
cardigan; dressing gown; blouse; skirt; leggings

6
a) 3   b) 5   c) 2   d) 6   e) 7   f) 4   g) 1

READING

7 2 D   3 C   4 E   5 A

8 2 F   3 T   4 T   5 T   6 F   7 F

WRITING

Spelling

9
2 goes   3 plays   4 buys   5 carries   6 does
7 washes   8 sells   9 wears   10 flies   11 writes

10
2 running   3 driving   4 going   5 flying
6 taking   7 playing   8 coming   9 swimming
10 stopping 11 having

PRONUNCIATION

Sound and spelling

11a)
2 A<u>me</u>rican
3 Br<u>a</u>zilian
4 a<u>ga</u>in
5 pict<u>u</u>re
6 moth<u>e</u>r
7 summ<u>e</u>r
8 train<u>e</u>rs
9 p<u>o</u>lice
10 of<u>te</u>n
11 Jap<u>a</u>nese
12 cardi<u>ga</u>n

DICTATION

Vocabulary

12
CLARE: Rebecca, someone has stolen my suitcase!
REBECCA: No! Are you sure?
CLARE: *It's* not in *my room*.
REBECCA: What was in it?
CLARE: *Most* of my *clothes*. I started to unpack my suitcase *last night*, but I was *tired* so I didn't *finish*.
REBECCA: Well, what do you need? I've got extra *jumpers* and *shorts* and *things*.
CLARE: Have you got an extra *swimming costume*?
REBECCA: No. But can't you wear *shorts* and a *T-shirt* to swim in?
CLARE: No, I can't, but I've got some *money*. I can buy *one*.
REBECCA: What clothes have you got?
CLARE: What I'm wearing; my *pyjamas* and this *cardigan*. Erm ... my *jeans*, my *cotton jacket* and the *shirt* and *skirt* I wore on the plane.
REBECCA: OK. We can go to the *shops* now, buy you a swimming costume and then go to the beach.

Unit 3

GRAMMAR

Present Simple or Past Simple?

1
2 Paula usually *plays* golf on Fridays, but last Friday she *played* squash with Jonathan.
3 Sarah and Sam usually *get up* at 8 am, but yesterday they *slept* until lunchtime.
4 Daniel usually *phones* his mother once a week, but last week he *phoned* her every evening because she *was* ill.
5 I usually *study* in the evenings, but last night I *watched* a great film on TV.

Past Simple or Past Continuous?

2a)
2 did   3 were playing   4 began   5 wanted   6 got
7 was riding   8 threw   9 fell   10 cut   11 left   12 ran
13 found   14 was talking   15 was telling   16 told
17 happened   18 said

3
2 When I *saw* John he *was talking* to the manager.
3 Sarah and Jack *were watching* TV when I *arrived*.

4 While Corinne *wasn't looking,* her daughter *ran* into the road.

5 I *was studying* when my sister *phoned.*

Prepositions of time

4

2 on   3 in, in   4 at, on   5 X   6 in   7 in

VOCABULARY

5

```
            1 J A P A N E S E
            2 M E X I C A N
            3 P I C A S S O
            4 S H I R T
        5 G L O V E S
            6 W I F E
    7 C A R D I G A N
        8 P A T I E N T
        9 H O N E S T
     10 B L A C K
     11 U N C L E
```

12 Nephew   Niece

6

1 Joe   2 sister   3 grandmother   4 uncle
5 brother-in-law   6 granddaughter

LISTENING

8a)

Anne Lombard
1 Age: 26
2 Position in the family: the youngest
3 Anne's sister is serious.
4 Anne's brother is friendly and fun-loving.
5 Anne is easygoing.

Brian Tellerman
1 Age: 23
2 Position in the family: an only child
3 Brian is generous and quiet.

Gillian Whitefield
1 Age: We don't know
2 Position in the family: middle child
3 Her brother doesn't like being alone.
4 Gillian's sister is often angry.
5 Gillian is easy-going and fun-loving.

WRITING

Linking words

9

2 but   3 so   4 because   5 but   6 so   7 and   8 because
9 so

DICTATION

Pronunciation

10a)

1 Jane's got *a* new boyfriend. His *name's* Peter.
2 *I'd* like *a* bottle *of* shampoo *and a* toothbrush, please.
3 *They're* buying *a* present *for* their mother.
4 I like walking. *I don't* need *a* car.
5 She *doesn't* want *a* cup *of* coffee.
6 *I've* got a letter *from* Jennifer.

Giving personal information

11

1 I was born on …
2 My favourite family member is …
3 The oldest member of my family is …
4 The youngest member of my family is …
5 I like my best friend because …

Unit 4

GRAMMAR

1a)

Permission: *can* and *can't*
2 Can I use the phone?
3 Can I have visitors?
4 Can I have pets?
5 Can I use the kitchen?
6 Can I have a bicycle?

b)

2 You can't have pets in the house.
3 You can't have visitors after 11 pm.
4 You can't cook at 1 am.
5 You can't put/keep your bicycle in the hall.

Obligation and advice

2

2 don't have to
3 should
4 must
5 don't have to
6 must
7 must

Can/could/may/could

3

2 a)   3 b)   4 a)   5 b)   6 b)

VOCABULARY

Clothes and jewellery

4

2 belt   3 ring   4 watch   5 earrings   6 gloves   7 trousers

Parts of the body, clothes and jewellery

5

2 ring   3 bracelet, watch   4 trousers, jeans, shorts, leggings
5 hat, scarf   6 shoes, trainers, boots, slippers, sandals, socks
7 necklace, scarf

You need a doctor!

6

2 sore throat   3 twisted   4 ached   5 felt   6 vitamins
7 cough   8 feet hurt

LISTENING

8a)

MIKE		DEBBIE	
✗	height	height	✓
✓	eyes	feet	✗
✓	nose	hair	✓
✗	ears	mouth	✗
✓	shape of face	legs	✓
		teeth	✗
		waist	✓

c)

3 Mike *likes* his nose because it's like his *father's/straight/small*.
4 Debbie *doesn't like* her feet because *they're big*.
5 Mike *doesn't like* his ears because *they're big*.
6 Debbie *likes* her hair because *it's easy to take care of*.
7 Debbie *likes* her waist because *it's small*.

WRITING

Spelling

9a)

2 and 3 and 4 but 5 because 6 because 7 and

b)

My room is *cheap* and *comfortable*.
This is a really *beautiful* and *interesting* island.
This makes everything look *attractive*.
The weather is always *sunny*.
I have to be *careful*.
The food is really *delicious*.

DICTATION

Sound and spelling /iː/

10a)

1 *The hotel's* very *cheap*, the food's great and I'm *eating* a lot.
2 I'm *leaving* for London next *week*.
3 I *need to* stop. My *feet are* hurting.
4 I *feel ill* today.
5 *Complete these* sentences.
6 *There are* lots of *people* on *the* bus.
7 My *niece* is *thirteen* tomorrow.

b)

1 cheap/eating
2 leaving/week
3 need/feet
4 feel
5 complete/these
6 There are/people/the
7 niece/thirteen

c)

ie	niece
ee	week, feet, feel, need, thirteen
ea	eating, cheap, leaving
eo	people
ete	complete
ese	these

Unit 5

GRAMMAR

Will or *going to*?

1

1 (2) She*'s going to have* an operation on her foot.
   (3) I'll *buy* her some magazines and chocolates.
   (4) I*'m going to leave* the offfice about six.
   (5) I*'ll bring* them to your office.
2 I*'ll go* and see it on Saturday.
3 (1) I*'ll buy* you a drink.
   (2) I*'ll give* you the money back tomorrow.

4 (1) Pete*'s going to get* a new job.
   (2) Who*'s* he *working* for?
   (3) I*'ll ask* Pat.

Will for offers, requests and decisions at the moment of speaking

2a)

2 b) 3 d) 4 f) 5 a) 6 c)

Future time using *will*, *going to* or the Present Continuous

3a)

2 going to get
3 'll take
4 'll ask
5 'll buy, 'll give
6 won't be

Will for offers and requests

4

3 Will you lend me some money for a taxi, please?
4 I'll carry your bag.
5 I'll take you to the station.
6 Will you switch on the light, please?
7 I'll make you a coffee/a cup of coffee/some coffee.

VOCABULARY

5

2 trip
3 journey
4 travelling
5 trip

6

Car	Boat	Plane
a windscreen	a cabin	to land
a brake	to sail	to take off
to brake	boarding card	seat belt
traffic lights		boarding card
stop sign		to fly
seat belt		
to drive		

7

2 noisy 3 wet 4 full 5 cheap

READING

9

2 No, she doesn't. She works for a TV company.
3 No, she didn't. There weren't any parking meters.
4 No, she didn't. Someone clamped the wheels on her car.
5 No, she didn't. She had to pay £58.

10

2 it = the road
3 it = her car
4 there = the road
5 they = people from the Camden Parking Ticket Office

WRITING

11

142 Amazonas
Quito
3 4 95

Dear Jean,

I love Quito, (1) *It* is wonderful. (2) *It* has new and old buildings which makes (3) *it* very interesting.

The people are really friendly, (4) *they* always try to help tourists. I have two lovely new Ecuadorian friends. I met (5) *them* on the first day I arrived. (6) *They* take me to beautiful new places every night.

The weather is beautiful too. (7) *It* isn't too hot and (8) *it* is never cold. I want to stay in Quito forever. (9) *It* is like home to me, but sadly I have to leave next week. See you soon.

Love Josephine

DICTATION

Pronunciation

12
1 They're early.
2 They're there, next to the TV.
3 That's their house there.
4 Well, their parents are rich.

Unit 6

GRAMMAR

Countable and uncountable nouns

1

Countable Nouns	Uncountable Nouns
journey/journeys	sugar
apple/apples	cream
potato/potatoes	luggage
pen/pens	furniture
newspaper/newspapers	milk
bottle/bottles	salt
toothbrush/toothbrushes	shampoo
stamp/stamps	toothpaste
	money
	food

2
2 some 3 any/some 4 some 5 any/some 6 a
7 any/some 8 some 9 some 10 a 11 some

Much/many/a lot (of)/a few/a little

3
2 b) 3 a) 4 a) 5 b) 6 b) 7 b) 8 a)

4 a)
2 much/any 3 some/a little 4 any/much 5 some
6 few 7 some 8 some 9 little 10 few 11 few
12 some 13 little 14 any 15 many/any 16 few
17 few 18 any

VOCABULARY

5

1	fish	5	orange	9	cheese
2	meat	6	strawberries	10	potato
3	banana	7	cauliflower	11	chicken
4	apple	8	yoghurt	12	lamb
				13	pasta

6
1 napkin G 2 dessert spoon I 3 knife K 4 fork H
5 plate J 6 cup L 7 mug E 8 saucer M 9 glass D
10 teaspoon N 11 candle C 12 salt and pepper pots A
13 bowl B 14 side plate F

LISTENING

7b)
David

7c)
2 T 3 T 4 F 5 T 6 T 7 F 8 T 9 T 10 F 11 F

PRONUNCIATION

8
1 walk 2 door 3 fourteen 4 saw/sore

9a)
water thought short tall floor morning

DICTATION

Contractions and weak forms

10
2 some 3 I'm 4 the 5 of 6 to 7 a 8 for 9 a
10 for 11 or 12 can 13 a 14 I'll 15 I'll 16 me
17 as 8 as 19 at

WRITING

Putting information in the correct order

11
This is only a **possible** answer. You might have something different which is **correct**.

First you get a train to Kingsbridge Station. After that you catch a number 22 bus to Pitney, and get off at the High Street. Next, you cross over the road. Then you walk up the hill. Finally you turn right into Bleaker Street.

Unit 7

GRAMMAR

Past Simple and past participles

1

Base form	Past Simple	Past participle
go	went	gone
tell	told	told
see	saw	seen
buy	bought	bought
give	gave	given
take	took	taken
send	sent	sent
drink	drank	drunk
eat	ate	eaten
have	had	had
think	. thought	thought

Present Perfect or Past Simple?

2
3   Have you ever been to Argentina?
4   Were you ill last week?
5   Have you finished the report yet?
6   Have you seen John?
7   Did you go to Dan's party on Saturday?
8   Have you seen Keanu Reeves' new film?

Been or *gone*?

3
2 been   3 gone   4 gone   5 been   6 gone

Present Perfect negatives

4
2   But we haven't read this one.
3   But she hasn't broken it.
4   But I haven't driven a Mercedes.
5   But they haven't bought any beer.
6   But I haven't told Ben.

Present Perfect or Past Simple?

5
2 She passed   3 Her mother's just bought
4 hasn't told   5 Have you bought

VOCABULARY

Adjectives and prepositions

6
2 of   3 with   4 with   5 about   6 about   7 in
8 with   9 for

READING

Finishing relationships

7b)
They do not talk about 3 and 4.

c)
2 F   3 T   4 F   5 T

WRITING

8a)
2 a   3 the   4 a   5 a   6 The   7 a   8 The   9 a
10 The   11 The   12 a   13 the   14 a   15 the

DICTATION

10a)
1   *Have* you *seen* my keys?
2   *Where did* you *buy* those shoes?
3   *Has* Peter *gone* to school yet?
4   *Did* you *like* the meal?
5   *Were* you ill yesterday?
6   *Was* David late on Monday?

Unit 8

GRAMMAR

To or *-ing*?

1

To + Base form	Base form + *-ing*
want	finish
hope	miss
promise	like
manage	
expect	
offer	
forget	
would like	

Note: The verbs *like* and *love* can be followed with *to* + base form or base form + *-ing* with only a very small change in meaning.

2a)
2 to go   3 to dive   4 being/to be   5 swimming/to swim
6 to arrange   7 to find   8 flying   9 to drive   10 to travel
11 to find   12 being   13 to sit/sitting

Adjectives and adjectives + prepositions

3
2 swimming   3 buying   4 to sleep   5 going   6 going   7 to
watch

4
2 with   3 at   4 with   5 about   6 from   7 for   8 at
9 of   10 with

VOCABULARY

Jobs

5a)
2 D   3 J   4 K   5 B   6 N   7 L   8 E   9 M   10 I   11 F   12 H
13 A   14 G

b)
1   engi'**neer**
2   '**jew**eller
3   '**gar**dener
4   'cook/'chef
5   li'**bra**rian
6   '**arch**itect
7   '**den**tist
8   '**dec**orator
9   '**scien**tist
10   '**law**yer
11   '**plum**ber
12   '**car**penter
13   elec'**tri**cian
14   '**sec**retary

6
2 take   3 post   4 plant   5 typed   6 decorate
7 designed (/decorated/built)   8 make

LISTENING

7a)

a) 1 a   2 b   3 b

8

2 a   3 a   4 a   5 b

9

2 They work 83 hours in a week.
3 She had 80 calls.
4 No, not in her free time.
5 No, they don't.
6 She's frightened of making a mistake.
7 Because she's tired.
8 Yes, she is.

PRONUNCIATION

Sound and spelling: *o*

10b)

/əʊ/	/aʊ/	/ʌ/	/ɒ/
broken	now	come	clock
throw	flower	money	lost
so	lovely	sock	
don't			
know			
snow			
go			

DICTATION

Names, dates, numbers and countries

11

Surname (1) <u>BROWNLY</u>
First name(s) (2) <u>TIMOTHY</u>
Mr/Mrs/Miss/Mrs (3) <u>Mr</u>   Age (4) <u>26</u>
Nationality (5) <u>Australian</u>
Address 16 (6) <u>Green</u>   St, (7) <u>London</u>   W1
Tel No (8) <u>0171 693 7062</u>

Previous experience as a waiter/waitress
McDonald's in (9) <u>Moscow</u>   1993-1994
Pasta Palace in (10) <u>New York</u>   (11) <u>1991</u>–1993
The Savoy in (12) <u>London</u>   1990–(13) <u>1991</u>

WRITING

A formal letter

12

6 The Manageress   5 **16 Green St**
   Angelo's Restaurant   **London W1**
   212 Piccadilly   2 **24 April**
   London W1

1 Dear Madam

9 Please find enclosed my application for the position of Head Waiter at Angelo's restaurant. I am also sending references from the managers of the Pasta Palace and The Savoy.

8 I have just returned from Moscow and as I am not working at the moment I could come for an interview any day during the week.

7 I look forward to hearing from you.

3 Yours faithfully

4 *Timothy Brownly*

Unit 9

GRAMMAR

Might, *will* and *won't*

1a)

1 2 won't fail   3 might pass   4 won't pass
2 1 might rain   2 won't rain   3 'll take   4 'll leave
3 1 'll be   2 'll be/might be
4 1 might go   2 won't want

First Conditional

2

2 g)   3 f)   4 a)   5 b)   6 e)   7 d)

First conditional and *might*

3

3 If I get ill, I'll find a doctor.
4 If I haven't got enough money, I'll get a job.
5 If I don't find a job, I'll ask you for more money.
6 If I don't like Paris, I'll come home.
7 If I get married, I'll invite you to the wedding.

First Conditional: negative sentences

4

2 If I *buy* that jacket, I *won't have* enough money for some trousers.
3 If you *dont want* to stay at the party, I*'ll take* you home.
4 If *you're* late, I *won't wait* for you.
5 If you *haven't got* time to write to me, *will you phone* me?
6 If he *doesn't like* wine, I'll buy some beer.
7 If we *don't leave*, we*'ll not catch* the train.
8 If it rains, I *won't play* tennis.

VOCABULARY

5

1 M   2 B   3 F   4 L   5 Q   6 J   7 E   8 N   9 P   10 H   11 C
12 G   13 A   14 I   15 K   16 D   17 O

PRONUNCIATION

6a)

'chair   'arm chair   'stool   'blinds   'cur tains   'shut ters
'rug   'car pet   'book shelf   'book case   'cup   'mug
'glass   'table   'dres sing table   'switch   'plug

b)
The first syllable.

LISTENING

7

This is only a **possible** answer. You may have a **different** answer which is **correct**.

Good things about **not** living in the city	Good things about living in the city
It's cleaner. There are fewer people. It's not as expensive. Life is slower.	There are more shops, theatres, restaurants and discos. Life is faster. There are always shops nearby. You don't need a car.

8b) LINDA = C, D, E, G, J
GRAHAM = A, C, F, H, I, J

c)
1 She thought it was too noisy, too dirty and there were too many people.
2 It is small and has only one bedroom.
3 She phones her father.
4 She is an artist.

d)
1 He works in a bank.
2 He doesn't have a car./ He can walk to anywhere he wants to go.
3 It's too expensive.
4 He'd like a dog.

WRITING

10a)
Joanna was walking through the *park* yesterday *afternoon* when she heard someone scream. The noise came from the lake so she ran as **fast** as she could and got to the lake very **quickly**. She saw *two* boys. The older boy was in the lake and the other one was standing by the side of the lake. Joanna **immediately** took off her jacket, jumped into the *lake* and swam to the boy in the water. When she got to him, he began to shout at her. Joanna turned the boy **carefully** on to his back and *swam* with him to where the younger boy was standing. She pulled the older boy onto the land and *sat* down.
'What are you doing?' asked the younger boy.
'I've just saved your friend's life,' said Joanna.
'But I wasn't in *danger,* I *can* swim!' said the older boy.
'Why did you scream so **loudly**?', asked Joanna.
'I didn't!' said the boy.
'I screamed,' said the younger boy. 'There was a bee on my *arm.'*

DICTATION

11
1 *If you don't get up*, we'll be late.
2 If we're late, *we won't catch the plane.*
3 If we don't catch the plane, *we won't have a holiday this year.*
4 If I don't have a holiday, *I'll go crazy!*
5 Look if you stop talking, *we won't be late!*

Unit 10

GRAMMAR: Revision of Units 1–9

1
2 are you coming 3 Does 4 Did 5 went 6 was eating
7 I'm wearing 8 will/'ll buy 9 Has 10 to buy
11 watching 12 reading 13 might come 14 I go

2
2 Where does Michelle work?
3 What time do you have to get up?
4 How many sisters has Sam got?
5 What did Gill buy last week?
6 Where will Janice stay if she comes to London?
7 Who lives in that house?
8 Where does Stephen live?

Questions and short answers

3
2 h) 3 g) 4 f) 5 a) 6 d) 7 b) 8 e) 9 c)

Word order: position of adverbs

4
2 I usually go to the cinema on Fridays.
3 I have just read this book.
4 (Sometimes) He (sometimes) leaves work early (sometimes).
6 I have not finished my homework yet.

VOCABULARY

5

In the house	Jobs
mug	pilot
stool	engineer
rug	politician
glass	mechanic
plug	
armchair	
sink	
dishwasher	

Things you wear	Parts of the body
belt	neck
trainers	wrist
gloves	fingers
zip	toes
socks	shoulder
bra	

READING

6b)

A	18	E	17
B	13	F	17
C	16	G	16/18
D	16	H	18

WRITING

7
Here is a **possible** answer. Your letter may be **different**. Check with your teacher if you have any questions.

167 Efroniou Street
Athens
Greece
31 July

Dear Mr and Mrs Staple, Alice and Sam

I arrived home on Friday, and the journey was fun because I travelled with a friend from college in England. It's good to be back with my family, but I miss you and all my friends in England very much. I want to thank you again for the wonderful time I had with you. You are a marvellous family.

When I unpacked my bags I couldn't find my English book. I think I left it in the cupboard in my bedroom at your house. It's really important because I wrote a lot of notes in it which I will need for my university course here in October. Could you send it to me, please? I hope this isn't too much trouble. I'll send a money order to pay for the postage.

I'm going to rest for a few days and then I'm going to work for my father until I start university in October.

Please write if you have time. I would love to have news about you all.

With best wishes from

Manolis

DICTATION

Sound and spelling: *c*

8
1 The *children* left a *cup* of *juice* on the *chair*.
2 *Can* you go to the *chemist* for me, and get my *medicine*?
3 I *can't decide* what to have for *lunch*?
4 I bought a *special cake* for tonight. It looks *delicious*.
5 I'm *certain* she's a *politician*.
6 There's been a terrible *car accident*.

9a)

/ k /	/ s /	/ tʃ /	/ ʃ /	/ ks /
chemist	twice	church	delicious	accident
car	juice	children	special	success
cake	medicine	cheap		
can	certain	kitchen		
electric		choose		
school		Charles		
actor				

Unit 11

GRAMMAR

Comparative and superlative adjectives

1
taller/tallest happier/happiest cheaper/cheapest more beautiful/most beautiful worse/the worst more horrible/most horrible dirtier/dirtiest lower/lowest higher/highest nicer/nicest better/best smaller/smallest more expensive/most expensive

2a)
2 The North Pole isn't as cold as the South Pole.
3 The black mamba is the fastest land snake in the world.
4 The most poisonous fish in the world is the box jellyfish.
5 The biggest tomato ever recorded was 1.9 kg.
6 The largest living thing in the world is a giant sequoia tree.

3 Three Sisters
2 bigger/biggest 3 lower/lowest 4 tallest/shortest
5 nicer/most beautiful 6 more attractive/most attractive

Comparing things

4a)
2 Well, he isn't as old as my grandmother.
3 Well, it isn't as dirty as mine.
4 Well, they aren't as nice as yours.
5 Well, he isn't as tall as Raymond.
6 Well, it isn't as expensive as The Ritz.
7 Well, it isn't as bad as *Monsters in New York*.

VOCABULARY

5
2 tennis 3 golf 4 squash 5 swimming

6
2 d) 3 b) 4 f) 5 a) 6 c) or e) 7 h) 8 g)

7a)
2 cyclist 3 swimmer 4 actress 5 dancer 6 cook
7 musician

READING

8
1 forty years ago 2 actors, musicians, sportsmen and women 3 7,000

9
1 He waits outside London theatres.
2 He goes to radio and television stations.
3 No, he doesn't.
4 He also goes to hotels.
5 More than £2,000,000.
6 $1,320,000.
7 It was President Abraham Lincoln's.

WRITING

Silent letters

11a)
Chri<u>st</u>mas <u>w</u>rite ri<u>gh</u>t <u>for</u> <u>k</u>nee eigh<u>t</u> school <u>gh</u>ost tal<u>k</u> <u>w</u>rong w<u>h</u>ich i<u>s</u>land Tu<u>e</u>sday We<u>d</u>ne<u>s</u>day

DICTATION

12
1 beautiful
2 neighbours
3 daughter
4 carried
5 written
6 awful

Unit 12

GRAMMAR

Second Conditional

1
2 If I knew the answer, I'd (would) tell you.
3 If I had £5, I'd lend it to you.
4 If I had time, I'd help you clean it.
5 If I caught the later train, I'd be late for work.

2a)

Here is a **possible** answer.

2 Oh, I wouldn't. I'd travel round the world.
3 Oh, I wouldn't. I'd be a film director.
4 Oh, I wouldn't. I'd choose Keanu Reeves.
5 Oh, I wouldn't. I'd go to America.

Giving advice

3a)

2 If I were you, I'd get some glasses.
3 If I were you, I'd put a plaster on it.
4 If I were you, I'd go to bed.
5 If I were you, I'd start exercising.
6 If I were you, I'd go to the dentist.
7 If I were you, I'd put those boxes down.

First or Second Conditional?

4

2 had/would take
3 don't put/'ll get
4 had/would get
5 'll leave/shouts
6 'll be/don't leave

VOCABULARY

5

2 examinations 3 advertisements 4 pronunciation
5 arguments 6 excitement 7 arrangements 8 decision
9 education 10 feelings

6a)

1 C 2 A 3 B 4 D

b)

B = autumn, C = summer, D = winter

WRITING

Punctuation

7

1 I'd give you a lift to London if I had time.
2 Please could you get me an aspirin?
3 John's not here now, but I can tell him on Friday.
4 Has anyone seen Cathy's keys?
5 If he came to the party, he'd enjoy himself.

LISTENING

8a)

4 9   5 5   6 7   7 11   8 10   9 8   10 6   11 12   12 4

c)

1 She's got three children.
2 She went to buy food for dinner.
3 About ten o'clock.
4 There is a window in the front door.
5 He ran out of the back door.
6 Mrs Stevens.
7 We don't know.

DICTATION

Grammar and pronunciation

9a)

1 She went home two hours ago.
2 I can take you to the station.

3 I'll take the children to school for you.
4 No, thanks. I have to go to work.
5 I'm going to the shops. I'll get you some.

b)

school, work

PRONUNCIATION

Sound and spelling: /v/ and /w/

10

1 white wine
2 someone quiet
3 very warm
4 lovely weather
5 quick question

Unit 13

GRAMMAR

Defining relative clauses

1

2 That's the woman who/that lives next door.
3 That's the girl who/that sold me the tickets.
4 I know a book which/that has all the answers.
5 I have a dog that/which likes music.
6 That's the shop where you can buy a good dictionary.
7 I know a man who/that has thirteen children.
8 She's a bank manager who/that works in Liverpool.

Directions

2

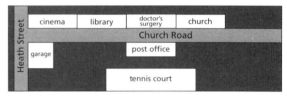

Adjectives: word order

3a)

2 large, round, wooden
2 small, square, yellow
4 black, leather
5 round, black, plastic
6 long, pink and white, cotton
7 short, orange, cotton

(We) use a _____ for _____ -ing

4

2 for making toast 3 for hanging up clothes 4 for washing
hair 5 for washing the floor 6 for measuring lines

VOCABULARY

Opposites

5a)

2 e) 3 g) 4 f) 5 d) 6 b) 7 a) 8 h)

b)

2 unfriendly 3 quiet 4 impatient 5 cheerful
6 mean 7 untidy 8 sociable 9 miserable

6

READING

7c)
2 to a restaurant (for a meal).
3 June had a boyfriend and Colin had a girlfriend.
4 she didn't love him.
5 he wanted to see June again.
6 an underground train (in London).
7 she felt sick/ill.
8 he helped her to get off the train.
9 she was sick all over Bob's shoes.
10 got a taxi for Janet.

PRONUNCIATION

Rhyming words

8
2 phone   3 glove   4 bed   5 so   6 late   7 taught   8 buy

WRITING

9
2 Her   3 Her   4 They   5 She's   6 her   7 They   8 we
9 she   10 He   11 her   12 He   13 her   14 Them   15 It
16 They   17 she

DICTATION

Vocabulary

10
1 Jane's got beautiful, long, straight, blonde hair.
2 Peter's not very tall. He's got a round face, brown eyes and lovely short, thick hair.
3 I bought a really expensive, long, red dress yesterday.
4 I like that small, round, wooden box. I could keep all my jewellery in it.
5 Susan's really lazy. She always leaves her clothes on the floor.

Unit 14

GRAMMAR

Used to and *didn't use to*

1a)
3 didn't use to exercise   4 go   5 used to ask   6 used to stay   7 don't eat   8 used to love   9 used to eat   10 eats

Past simple or *used to*?

2a)
We cannot use *used to* in 1, 3, 5, 6.

b)
1 Last week I smoked a lot of cigarettes.
3 I bought an old car. I paid £50 for it.
5 We got our first TV when I was twelve.
6 I'm tired, and I slept for ten hours last night.

Question tags

3
2 e)   3 g)   4 b)   5 f)   6 a)   7 d)

Time expressions

4
2 **in** the afternoon.   3 correct   4 correct   5 **at** 2pm
6 **in** winter   7 correct   8 **last** month (no preposition)
9 correct

VOCABULARY

Entertainment

5
1 cassette recorder   2 camcorder   3 headphones
4 video recorder   5 cassette   6 CD

6
2 booked   3 front row   4 programme   5 acting
6 stage   7 clapped   8 audience   9 interval
10 performance

7a)
2 E   3 B   4 F   5 G   6 D   7 A

b)
1 **'sax**ophone   2 pi'**an**o   3 gui'**tar**   4 '**flute**   5 clari'**net**
6 '**drums**   7 vio'**lin**

LISTENING

8b)
1 Sally   2 Carol   3 Marc and Carol   4 Sally

c)
3 Marc plays in a group that plays rock and reggae music.
8 Carol likes classical music.
9 Carol enjoys staying at home and reading.
11 Sally likes art galleries.
12 There aren't many free art galleries.
13 Sally hasn't got much money.
14 Sally doesn't have a video recorder.

WRITING

Adverbs

9
2 quickly   3 slowly   4 quickly   5 angrily   6 very well
7 carefully   8 quietly   9 patiently

DICTATION

Sound and spelling: *a*

10a)
1 *What* do you *want* from the *bank*?
2 I have to go now. But on *Saturday* I can *talk* to you *all* day.
3 I can't *stay*. I'll have to *wait* if I miss my *train*.
4 I'm *happy* that you *passed* your *exams*.
5 John's very *fast*. He was the first in the *race*, but I was *last*.

11

/ɒ/	/æ/	/eɪ/	/ɔː/	/ɑː/
want	bank	made	fall	car
	Saturday	late	talk	
	sad		wall	
	bad		ball	
	exam			
	fan			

Unit 15

GRAMMAR

Someone, anyone, no one, everyone, something, anything, nothing and *everything*

1

2 nothing   3 No one   4 Everyone   5 no one   6 someone
7 something   8 someone   9 anyone   10 anyone
11 everyone   12 Everything

Too much or *too many?*

2

2 too much   3 too much   4 too many   5 too much
6 too many   7 too much

Correct the mistakes

3

1 some   2 anyone   everyone   3 Someone   4 No one
5 nothing   6 something   7 too much
8 too many   someone

VOCABULARY

4a)

2 pass   study   3 do   4 attend   fail   5 pass   go   get

British English and American English

5a)

2 c)   3 e)   4 f)   5 a)   6 b)   7 h)   8 g)

b)

2 private school   3 pharmacy/drugstore   4 purse
5 pharmacy/drugstore   6 gas   7 gas station   8 gas   9 purse
10 wallet   11 pants

READING

6b)

C, E, B, A

c)

2 No, she didn't.   3 No, she didn't.   4 No, she didn't.

d)

2   they didn't want their mothers to leave.
3   stand up, put their hands together close their eyes (for prayers).
4   she didn't close her eyes.
5   the teacher shouted at her.

WRITING

Linking words

7

2 Although   3 also   4 but   5 because   6 so   7 However

DICTATION

Vocabulary and word stress

8

1   I *want to go to university and study economics.*
2   John *passed his geography exam but he failed literature.*
3   I *studied physics and chemistry at university.*
4   Jennifer's *studying law and politics this year.*

9

1   'politics   2   poli'tician   3   po'litical
4   eco'nomics   5   e'conomist   6   eco'nomical
7   e'lectric   8   elec'trician   9   elec'tricity

Unit 16

GRAMMAR

Passives

1

3 are made in   4 is/was made of   5 is made in   6 are made
of   7 are/were made in   8 was made in   9 was made in

2

Past Simple
2 projected   3 called   4 gave   5 began   6 were
7 became
Past Simple Passive
2 was built   3 were shown   4 was built   5 were made
6 was shown   7 was called

3a)

2   Who built the cinematographe?
3   What was the machine called?
4   When was the first public film shown?
5   Where was the first cinema built?
6   When was the first talkie made?
7   When did filmmakers begin to use actors?

4

2   The towels are washed every day.
3   The rooms are cleaned every day.
4   Only fresh food is used.
5   Breakfast is brought to your room.
6   Our customers are given the best service.

VOCABULARY

Negatives

5

2 disagree   3 unhappy   4 incorrect   5 unkind   6 untidy
7 inexperienced   8 dissatisfied

Words and spelling

6

2a) pear b) pair   3a) rode b) Road   4a) there b) their
5a) one b) won   6a) nose b) knows

LISTENING

7a)

1 B   2 C   3 A

b)

2 No, they weren't.   3 Yes, she did.   4 Yes, they were.
5 No, they weren't.   6 No, she wasn't.   7 Yes, it did.
8 No, it didn't.   9 Yes, she was.   10 Yes, she was.
11 No, she wasn't.   12 No, it isn't.   13 Yes, they did.
14 Yes, they did.   15 Yes, they were.

WRITING

Punctuation

8

2 Two men wearing black, leather coats ran into the bank with guns.
3 The bank manager said, 'The two men shouted at us all and told us all to sit on the floor with our hands on our heads.'
4 The two men put £30,000 into a red suitcase and ran out of the building.
5 However, the suitcase wasn't closed properly so all the money fell out onto the street.
6 The two men were caught while they were trying to pick the money up.

DICTATION

Passives

9

1 President Abraham Lincoln was killed by an *actor*.
2 The telephone was invented by A. G. Bell in *1876*.
3 Paper was invented by the *Chinese*.
4 Photography was invented in the *1840s*.
5 The Statue of Liberty was given to the American people by the *French* government.
6 The Taj Mahal in India was built by Shah Jahan for his favourite *wife* who died in 1631.

Unit 17

GRAMMAR

Present Perfect Simple and Continuous

1

2 since   3 for   4 for   5 since   6 for   7 since   8 since
9 for   10 for

2

2 Has he been working here since Christmas?
3 Have they had their car for long?
4 How long have you known Peter?
5 Who has been eating my chocolate?
6 How long has Mary had that new sports car?
7 Have you been waiting for us for long?
8 Have you seen my car key?

3

2 been   3 had   4 been   5 known   6 doing   7 finished
8 washed   9 borrowing   10 borrowing   11 given   12 been

4

2 He's walked   3 I've read   4 I've been reading
5 She's been writing   6 She's written

VOCABULARY

5

2 photographer   3 electrical   4 patient   5 decision
6 choose   7 medical   8 dead   9 married   10 robbery

6

	Adjective	Adverb	Noun	Verb
1	interested	interestedly	interest	–
2	safe	safely	safety	–
3	friendly	–	friend	–
4	–	–	robber/robbery	rob
5	happy	happily	happiness	–
6	worried	worriedly	worry	worry
7	photographic	– photographically	photography/ photographer	photograph

LISTENING

7b)
2 No, he doesn't.   3 No, he isn't.

c)
2 T   3 F   4 T   5 T

d)
1 cooking, washing up, tidying up
2 Because they ate too much.
3 They are bad-tempered. They push and shout.
4 Shaving cream.
5 He's got a beard./He doesn't shave.
6 He's going to work.

WRITING

Paragraphs

8

Paragraph 1 begins: Thank you ...
2 begins: I hope...
3 begins: University starts ...
4 begins: I have to ...

Improving the letter

9a)

Positive		Negative
great	wonderful	awful
excellent	interesting	bad
good	brilliant	dreadful
delicious	lovely	terrible
	fantastic	

b)
Nice can be replaced by the positive adjectives, with *interesting* for the photography course, and *delicious* for the food. The negative adjectives can all replace *not nice*. If you have any questions, please ask your teacher.

DICTATION

Contrastive stress

10a)

1 A: The bus leaves at '**eight** o'clock.
  B: No, the '**train** leaves at eight o'clock. The bus leaves at '**ten**.

2 A: Did you ask for '**coff**ee?
  B: No, '**John** asked for coffee. I asked for '**tea**.

3 A: John bought a blue and white striped '**jum**per.
  B: No, he bought a blue and '**yellow** striped jumper.

4 A: We're going to New York to'**day**.
  B: I'm going to New York on '**Wed**nesday.

Unit 18

GRAMMAR

Sentence patterns and reported sentences

1
1   He asked me not to make any noise after 11 pm.
3   They told me not to tell anyone.
4   She asked me to open the window.
5   Tom told me to stop work.
6   Sylvia asked me to drive Steve to the party.
7   They asked me not to smoke in this room.
8   Francis told me to come back again in an hour.
9   The doctor told me not to give Nicholas anything to drink.

2b)
2   I said *I knew he was very unhappy here.*
3   Then David said Jim *didn't like his manager.*
4   I told *him that was because his manager was a woman.*
5   Then David told me *Jim was going to apply for a new job in America.*
6   I said *there were more women managers in America than in England.*
7   Then David told *me not to tell Jim.*

3
 4   I wanted **to** buy you some flowers, but I couldn't find any.
 6   He decided not **to** change his job.
 7   I want **to** ask you a question.
11   He **told** me Jane was ill/He **said** Jane was ill.
12   I finished **working** at seven o'clock last night.
The other sentences are correct.

VOCABULARY

Phrasal verbs

4a)
2 g)   3 h)   4 f)   5 a)   6 i)   7 e)   8 b)   9 d)   10 j) or d)

b)
2 run away   3 Hold on   4 took off   5 turned up
6 given up   7 come over   come round   8 bring back

Do or *make*?

5
2 do   3 do   4 make   5 make   6 make

DICTATION

7
1   Betty was tall and slim, *but she wasn't very good looking.*
2   Betty *was forty years old.*
3   The young man *was twenty-two years old.*
4   It's *the beginning of a murder story.*

PRONUNCIATION

Sound and spelling: *u*

9

/ʌ/	/ʊ/	/ɜː/	/uː/	/juː/
under	full	nurse		uniform
must	put	church		usual
cup		hurt		university
button				
umbrella				
lunch				
unhappy				

Unit 19

GRAMMAR

If or *unless*?

1
2 b)   3 a)   4 b)   5 b)   6 a)   7 a)   8 b)   9 b)   10 a)

Verb patterns 1

2a)
2 'll/will be   3 look   4 'll/will see   5 'll/will start   6 want
7 arrives   8 'll/will go   9 haven't got   10 'll/will buy
11 'll/will give   12 opens

Verb patterns 2

3
3   Jim bought Rebecca some flowers.
4   Sam read a story to his son.
5   We will take Mary some tea.
6   Please take it to Mary.
7   Please show James this picture.
8   I gave the bag to John.
9   Can you pass me the salt, please?

VOCABULARY

Spelling

4a)
2 football   3 beat   4 course   5 track   6 goal   7 racket
8 court   9 throw

b)
2 scored   3 went   4 basketball   5 kick   6 Catch   7 golf
8 boxing

LISTENING

5a)
1 G   2 F   3 C   4 E   5 D   6 A   7 B

6
Picture 2 is not from the story.

a)
2 drive (to the mountains)   3 advanced/very good/excellent
4 children   5 leg/knee   6 girl   7 blood/hurt   8 leg
9 hospital

WRITING

Punctuation

7
1   Mrs Evans walked into the living room where her husband was watching TV.
2   'Not another football match,' she said. 'That's the third today.'
3   Mr Evans told his wife to be quiet.
4   'You don't need to watch a football match,' said Mrs Evans.
5   'OK, but I don't want to watch you,' said her husband.
6   Mrs Evans went to the kitchen and took a large kinfe from the drawer.

DICTATION

Rhythm and sentence stress

8a)
1 Where did she go?
2 Did he see her?
3 What did she do?
4 Is he dead?
5 Did the police find the knife?
6 Did she kill him?
7 Did they catch her?
8 Did the police find her?

b)
2 b) 3 a) 4 b) 5 b) 6 b) 7 a) 8 a)

Unit 20

GRAMMAR

1
2 My sister isn't as tall as me.
3 If I had more time, I'd go to the cinema more often.
4 If I didn't smoke, I'd have more money.
5 It's a big, brown leather bag.
6 There's the shop where I bought my book.
7 Yesterday I went to the shop.
8 He works here, doesn't he?
9 There's someone at the door.
10 There's too much sugar in my tea.
11 The murderer was taken to prison.
12 They were given two free tickets for the theatre.
13 I've known John for ten years.
14 I've been learning English for two years.
15 He asked me to go to his office at 10 am.
16 Unless we clean up our mess, Mum will be angry.
17 I gave John the money for the tickets. / I gave the money for the tickets to John.
18 As soon as she arrives, we'll call for a taxi.

Comparatives

2a)
2 The Hilton is more expensive than this hotel.
3 The beaches in England are cleaner than they used to be.
4 Rian's restaurant is cheaper than Brown's.
5 Last week the weather was worse than it was this week.

3
2 went 3 had 4 have had 5 have decided 6 to visit
7 arrive 8 will go 9 were designed 10 used to spend
11 walking 12 to spend 13 could 14 would study
15 am going 16 have known 17 were 18 will be
19 will learn

VOCABULARY

4
2 impossible 3 disagree 4 unsafe 5 untidy
6 uncomfortable 7 unnecessary 8 unpopular 9 unlucky
10 incomplete

5
2 education 3 excitement 4 decision 5 discussion
6 enjoyment 7 examination

6

LISTENING

7b)
Sentences 1 and 4 are correct.

c)
2 How did they get/travel to Turkey?
3 Why did he fail his exams?
4 How long did they stay in Turkey/there?

d)
2 Because he wanted money for the holiday.
3 In the van.
4 No, they didn't.
5 Yes, it did.
6 No, they didn't.
7 Walking on the beach, swimming and playing football.

WRITING

Linking words

8a)
2 so 3 because 4 and 5 However, 6 and 7 when
8 When 9 and 10 and 11 However, 12 because
13 and 14 so 15 Then 16 and 17 but

DICTATION

Sound and spelling: g

9a)
1 I gave Paul an orange.
2 The judge wanted to see the gun.
3 Let me look at that page.
4 The weather's changed. It's foggy now.

b)

Silent 'g'	/g/	/dʒ/
bright	garden	Gillian
light	pig	orange
foreign	gun	judge
	fog	page
	again	change
	ugly	large
	Gary	fridge
	goal	George
		bridge
		agent

Enjoying life

GRAMMAR

Comparative and superlative adjectives

1 Complete the table.

Adjective	Comparative	Superlative
big	_bigger_ than	the _biggest_
tall	_____ than	the _____
happy	_____ than	the _____
cheap	_____ than	the _____
beautiful	_____ than	the _____
bad	_____ than	the _____
horrible	_____ than	the _____
dirty	_____ than	the _____
low	_____ than	the _____
high	_____ than	the _____
nice	_____ than	the _____
good	_____ than	the _____
small	_____ than	the _____
expensive	_____ than	the _____

2 a) All these facts are _true_, but there are some mistakes with the comparative and superlative forms in these sentences. Correct the mistakes.

1 The Amazon is _widest_ river in the world.

   The Amazon is _the widest_ river in the world.

2 The North Pole isn't as colder as the South Pole.

   _____

   _____

3 The black mamba is the most fast land snake in the world. It can move at 25 km per hour.

   _____

   _____.

4 The poisonous fish in the world is the box jellyfish which can kill a person in 30 seconds.

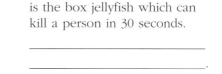

   _____

   _____.

5 The most biggest tomato ever recorded was 1.9kg.

   _____

   _____.

6 The most large living thing in the world is a giant sequoia tree. It's 83 metres tall and 24.11 metres round.

   _____

   _____

   _____.

b) [🔲 11.1]   Listen and check your answers.

3 Three Sisters

	Barbara	Jane	Clare
Salary	£20,000	£7,000	£12,000
Flat	3 bedrooms	2 bedrooms	1 bedroom
Rent	£300	£100	£150
	per month	per month	per month
Height	1.60 metres	1.80 metres	1.85 metres
Hair	OK	beautiful	nice
Husbands	very, very attractive	attractive	very attractive

Read the information about Barbara, Jane and Clare and complete these sentences. Use the adjectives in brackets.

1 (_high_) (_low_)   Barbara has the _highest_ salary, and Jane has the _lowest_ salary.

2 (_big_)   Jane's flat is _____ than Clare's, but Barbara's flat is the _____.

3 (*low*) Clare's rent is _____ than Barbara's, but Jane's rent is the _____.

4 (*tall*) (*short*) Clare is the _____, and Barbara is the _____.

5 (*nice*) (*beautiful*) Clare's hair is _____ than Barbara's, but Jane's hair is the _____.

6 (*attractive*) Clare's husband is _____ than Jane's, but Barbara's husband is the _____.

Comparing things

4 a) Make sentences with *not as* + adjective + *as*.

1 A: Peter's the richest person I know.

B: (*Sarah*) *Well, he isn't as rich as Sarah!*

2 A: Your grandfather's the oldest person I know.

B: (*my grandmother*) _____

3 A: John's flat is the dirtiest place I've seen.

B: (*mine*) _____

4 A: Those are the nicest shoes I've seen.

B: (*yours*) _____

5 A: Ian's the tallest man I know.

B: (*Raymond*) _____

6 A: My hotel is really expensive!

B: (*The Ritz*) _____

7 A: I saw *Horror in Texas* last night. It's a really bad film.

B: (*Monsters in New York*) _____

b) [🔈 11.2] Listen and check your answers.

VOCABULARY

5 Verbs and nouns. Which noun does NOT go with the verb on the left?

Verbs	Nouns
1 take	pain~~t~~ings photos
2 go	swimming riding running tennis
3 collect	stamps autographs golf
4 do	squash exercises crosswords
5 play	games cards football swimming golf tennis

6 Compound nouns. Match a word from A with a word from B to make a new noun.

A	**B**
1 hair	a) box
2 photograph	b) glasses
3 sun	c) paste
4 swimming	d) album
5 post	e) brush
6 tooth	f) costume
7 air	g) case
8 suit	h) port

7 a) Complete this conversation.

OLIVER: I'm in love, Patrick! With a fantastic woman.

PATRICK: Where did you meet her?

OLIVER: I met her on a skiing holiday. She's a really good (*skiing*) (1) _skier_.

PATRICK: So she likes sport.

OLIVER: Oh, yes. She's a great (*cycling*) (2) _____, and a good (*swimming*) (3) _____.

PATRICK: She sounds wonderful. What does she do?

OLIVER: She's studying dance and drama. She wants to be an (*acting*) (4) _____ or perhaps a (*dancing*) (5) _____. She's not sure.

PATRICK: Well, she sounds perfect. Is she a good (*cooking*) (6) _____?

OLIVER: She's the best! And she's a great (*music*) (7) _____, too.

PATRICK: Marry her. Today!

OLIVER: There is one little problem.

PATRICK: What's that?

OLIVER: She can't speak English. I can't speak German!

PATRICK: Oh. Yes, a little problem.

b) [🔈 11.3] Listen and check your answers.

READING

8 Read the article about Gordon Alford, an autograph collector. Complete these sentences.

1 Gordon Alford got his first autograph _____.

2 He collects the autographs of _____.

3 He now has _____ autographs.

LOOKING FOR NAMES

Forty years ago Gordon Alford was on holiday when he decided to ask some famous footballers for their autographs.

Since that time he has collected 7,000 autographs. He has thirteen specially-made albums for them. Most of his autographs are from famous actors, musicians and sportsmen and women.

Gordon often leaves the house before seven in the morning to go and stand outside radio and television stations. He waits to catch anyone famous coming in or going out.

In the evening he waits outside London theatres. 'I go two hours before the show begins and wait outside the stagedoor where the actors go in.' He also returns when the show has finished and waits for them to come out, or finds out which hotel they are staying at and waits there.

Some autographs are worth a lot of money. For example, an autograph from any of The Beatles (a very famous rock 'n' roll group in the 1960s) is worth £1,500.

The highest price anyone has paid for an autograph is $1,320,000, which was for President Abraham Lincoln's signature. And the autograph that every collector would love to have is the signature of William Shakespeare, the famous English writer who died in 1616. A collector could pay more than two million pounds for his signature.

(from *You*)

9 Read the article again and answer these questions.

1 Where does Gordon spend most evenings? _____.

2 Where does Gordon go so early in the morning? _____.

3 Does he spend all evening outside theatres? _____.

4 Apart from theatres, radio and television stations what other places does he go to?_____.

5 How much money could a collector pay for William Shakespeare's signature?_____.

6 What is the most money that anyone has paid for an autograph?

_____.

7 Whose autograph was it? _____.

WRITING

Spelling

10 Good spellers can see words in their heads. English spelling is often not the same as the pronunciation. Sometimes it's easier to remember what the word looks like.

Look at the words on the left. Then cover them with a piece of paper. Look at the different spellings on the right. Which one looks correct?

certain	certen	certin	(certain)
definitely	definately	definitely	definitly
experience	eksperience	experiance	experience
Tuesday	Tuesday	Tusday	Tuasday
Wednesday	Wensday	Wedensday	Wednesday
their	their	ther	thier
niece	niece	neece	neice
February	February	Febry	Febuary
medicine	medecine	medicine	medicin
language	languge	langage	language
different	differant	different	diffrent
complete	complete	compleat	compleet

11 Silent letters

a) Underline the letter or letters which we do NOT pronounce.

lis<u>t</u>en Christmas write right for knee eight school ghost talk wrong which island Tuesday Wednesday

b) [📼 11.4] Listen and check your answers.

c) Look at the words. Try to remember what they look like and which letters we do not pronounce. Cover the words with a piece of paper. Then listen again and write the words down.

DICTATION

Spelling and the alphabet

12 [📼 11.5] Listen to the spelling of the missing words. Then complete the sentences.

1 Her cat is really _____.

2 Do you like your _____?

3 Is that your _____?

4 He _____ his son to the car.

5 She's _____ four letters this morning.

6 Jonathan's got an _____ cold.

Witness

GRAMMAR

Second Conditional

1 Use the words in brackets to write B's answers. Use the Second Conditional.

1 A: I really like those boots.

  B: (have enough money/buy them for you)

    If *I had enough money, I'd buy them for you.*

2 A: Please tell me the answer.

  B: (know the answer/tell you)

    If _____ .

3 A: Can I borrow £5?

  B: (have £5/lend it to you)

    If _____ .

4 A: This room is a mess!

  B: (have time/help you clean it)

    If _____ .

5 A: Why do you always get up so early?

  B: (catch the later train/be late for work)

    If _____ .

2 a) Disagree with these statements. Use the Second Conditional negative.

1 A: If I had a choice, I'd live in Scotland.

  B: *Oh, I wouldn't. I'd live in Canada.*

2 A: If I had lots of money, I'd buy a big house.

  B: Oh, I _____ .

3 A: If I could have any job, I'd be a pilot.

  B: Oh, I _____ .

4 A: If I could meet a famous person, I'd choose Steven Spielberg.

  B: Oh, I _____ .

5 A: If I could have a holiday, I'd go to Kenya.

  B: Oh, I _____ .

b) [📼 12.1]   Listen and compare your answers.

Giving advice

3 a) We often use *If I were you, I'd ...* when we want to give advice. Choose the best advice from the box for the problems.

> call the doctor   put those boxes down
> go to the dentist   get some glasses
> start exercising   go to bed   put a plaster on it

1 Problem – A: I've got a temperature and I feel really ill.

  Advice – B: *If I were you, I'd call the doctor.*

2 A: This is too small. I can't read it.

  B: _____ .

3 A: Oh, I've cut my finger on this knife.

  B: _____ .

4 A: I'm really tired.

  B: _____ .

5 A: I'm getting fat. My jeans don't fit me.

  B: _____ .

6 A: I've got a terrible toothache.

  B: _____ .

7 A: My back is hurting.

  B: _____ .

b) [📼 12.2]   Listen and check your answers.

First or Second Conditional?

4 Complete these conversations with a First or a Second Conditional verb form.

1 A: I can play the guitar, but I can't read music.

   B: If you (*want*) *want* to learn, I'm sure my brother (*teach*) *will teach* you.

2 A: I feel really ill today.

   B: If I (*have*) _____ my car, I (*take*) _____ you home, but I came to work by train today.

3 A: I love lying in the sun!

   B: Be careful! If you (*not put*) _____ suncream on, you (*get*) _____ burnt.

4 A Have you got any pets?

   B: No, but if I (*have*) _____ a garden, I (*get*) _____ a dog.

5 A What's the matter?

   B: It's the manager. He always shouts at me. I (*leave*) _____ if he (*shout*) _____ at me again.

6 A: I can't find my briefcase!

   B: Look at the time! You (*be*) _____ late for work if you (*not leave*) _____ soon.

VOCABULARY

5 Make nouns from the verbs in brackets. Then complete these sentences. Some nouns must be plural.

1 (*meet*)   Are you coming to the *meeting*?
2 (*examine*)   I have to study tonight. I've got two _____ tomorrow.
3 (*advertise*)   I think they should stop making tobacco _____.
4 (*pronounce*)   Your English _____ is excellent, Juan.
5 (*argue*)   Please! No more _____ at the dinner table.
6 (*excite*)   Jane won a lot of money. All the _____ made her ill.
7 (*arrange*)   I've made all the _____ for the holiday.

8 (*decide*)   I can't make a _____ now. I'll tell you this afternoon.
9 (*educate*)   I want a good _____ for my children.
10 (*feel*)   That woman hasn't got any _____. She's horrible to me.

6 a) What's the weather like?
Match the descriptions with the pictures.

1 It's sunny. __
2 It's raining. __
3 It's cloudy. __
4 It's freezing. __

A

B

C   D

b) Which season (spring, summer, autumn, winter) is each picture?

A = *spring* _____

WRITING

Punctuation

7 Punctuate these sentences with full stops (.), question marks (**?**), commas (**,**), and apostrophes ('). Don't forget to use capital letters where necessary.

1 id give you a lift to london if i had time
   I'd give you a lift to London if I had time.

2 please could you get me an aspirin

   _____

3 johns not here now but i can tell him on friday

   _____

4 has anyone seen cathys key

   _____

5 if he came to the party hed enjoy himself

   _____

LISTENING

8 a) This morning a man burgled Mrs Daniel's house. These are the things that happened, but they are in the wrong order. What do you think is the correct order? Numbers 1–3 happened first and 13 happened last.

1 Mrs Daniels left the house at 8 am.   _1_
2 She took her older children to school.   _2_
3 She went to the shops with her baby.   _3_
4 She ran to the back garden.   ___
5 She saw a man in her house.   ___
6 The neighbour and the burglar heard her scream.   ___
7 The neighbour saw the man.   ___
8 The man jumped over the wall and ran away.   ___
9 The man ran out of the back door of the house.   ___
10 Mrs Daniels screamed.   ___
11 The neighbour called the police.   ___
12 She went home.   ___
13 The neighbour made Mrs Daniels a cup of tea.   _13_

b) [12.3] Listen and check your answers.

c) Listen again and answer these questions.

1 How many children has Mrs Daniels got?

_____

2 Why did she go to the shops?

_____

3 What time did she get home?

_____

4 How could she see the man in the hall?

_____

5 When she screamed, what did the burglar do?

_____

6 Who saw the burglar's face, Mrs Daniels or Mrs Stevens?

_____

7 Did the man take anything?

_____

DICTATION

Grammar and pronunciation

9 a) [12.4] Listen and write the answers to these sentences.

1 Where's Maggie?

_____

2 Hurry! We'll be late.

_____

3 I feel really ill.

_____

4 Do you want another coffee?

_____

5 I need some sugar.

_____

b) The definite article. Look at the sentences you wrote. Circle the places that do **not** need *the*.

1 (home)   2 station   3 school
4 work   5 shop

PRONUNCIATION

Sound and spelling: /v/ and /w/

10 [12.5] Usually the sounds /v/ and /w/ are spelt with the letters *v* and *w*. However, words like *one* /wʌn/ also have a /w/ sound. Listen and write what you hear.

1 _____
2 _____
3 _____
4 _____
5 _____

Love is all around

GRAMMAR

1 Defining relative clauses

Join these sentences with *who*, *where*, *which* or *that*. Remember *who* or *that* is for people, *where* is for places, *which* or *that* is for things.

1 That's the disco. I met my boyfriend there.

That's the disco where I met my boyfriend.

2 That's the woman. She lives next door.

_____

_____.

3 That's the girl. She sold me the tickets.

_____

_____.

4 I know a book. It has all the answers.

_____

_____.

5 I have a dog. It likes music.

_____.

6 That's the shop. You can buy a good dictionary there.

_____

_____.

7 I know a man. He has thirteen children.

_____

_____.

8 She is a bank manager. She works in Liverpool.

_____

_____.

Directions

2 Write the names of the places in italics in the correct box on the map.

1 The *cinema* is on the corner of Heath St and Church Rd, opposite the garage.
2 Next to the cinema there is a *library*.
3 Between the church and the library there's a *doctor's surgery*.
4 Opposite the surgery there's a *post office*.
5 Behind the post office there's a *tennis court*.

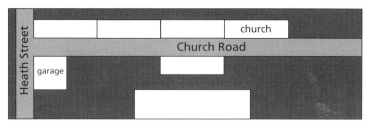

Adjectives: word order

3 a) Read the conversation in a furniture shop. Put the adjectives in brackets in the correct order.

SHOP ASSISTANT: Can I help you sir?

1 CUSTOMER: Yes. I'd like a (*plastic/ yellow/round/small*) <u>small, round, yellow, plastic</u> table, please.

2 SHOP ASSISTANT: I'm very sorry, sir. We only have a (*wooden/large/ round*) _____ table. But you can paint it yellow.

CUSTOMER: Yes, but I can't make it smaller!

3 SHOP ASSISTANT: Well, we have got a (*small/square/yellow*) _____ table.

4 CUSTOMER: OK. I'll have that. I also need four (*leather/black*) _____ chairs.

5 SHOP ASSISTANT: I'm very sorry, sir. We only have these (*plastic/round/black*) _____ stools, but they're very cheap.

48

6 CUSTOMER: OK. I also need some (*pink and white/cotton/long*) _____ curtains.

7 SHOP ASSISTANT: I'm very sorry, sir. We've only got (*orange/cotton/short*) _____ curtains in this shop.

CUSTOMER: OK. I'll take those, please.

b) [🔲 13.1] Listen and check your answers.

(We) use a ____ for ____ -ing

4 Complete these sentences using the verb in brackets and a noun from the box.

| the floor lines hair papers clothes toast |

Remember to use the preposition *for* and use the *-ing* form of the verb.

1 We use a briefcase *for carrying papers*. (*carry*)
2 We use a toaster _____. (*make*)
3 We use a wardrobe _____. (*hang up*)
4 We use shampoo _____. (*wash*)
5 We use a mop _____. (*wash*)
6 We use a ruler _____. (*measure*)

VOCABULARY

Opposites

5 a) Match the words in A with their opposites in B.

A	**B**
1 lively	a) untidy
2 hardworking	b) mean
3 patient	c) quiet
4 friendly	d) miserable
5 cheerful	e) lazy
6 generous	f) unfriendly
7 tidy	g) impatient
8 shy	h) sociable

b) Complete these sentences with one of the words from Exercise 5a).

1 Michael never does any work. He's very *lazy*.
2 John never says hello to anyone. He's very _____.
3 Mary doesn't talk very much. She's very _____.
4 Don hates waiting for anything. He's very _____.
5 Laura laughs all the time. She's very _____.
6 Lillian's got a lot of money, but she never buys anyone a present. She's very _____.
7 Peter never cleans his room. He's very _____.
8 Damian loves meeting new people. He's very _____.
9 Pauline's always unhappy. She's very _____.

6 Put the opposites of these words in the crossword.

ACROSS	DOWN
2 in front of	1 tall
4 noisy	3 out
7 off	5 pretty
8 young	6 stupid
10 short	9 wrong
11 fat	12 fair
13 asleep	14 ill
15 expensive	
16 fast	

READING

7 a) Before you read the articles, think about a married couple you know. Where did they meet?

b) Read these articles about two couples.

c) Complete these sentences about June and Janet.

1 June met Colin at a _jazz concert_.

2 After the concert June and Colin went _____ _____.

3 They didn't see each other again until 31 December because _____ _____.

4 June finished her relationship with Kenny because _____ _____.

5 Colin planned the party because _____ _____.

6 Janet met Bob on _____ _____.

7 Janet stood up to get off the train because _____ _____.

8 Bob knew Janet wasn't well so _____ _____.

9 Janet was embarrassed because _____ _____.

10 Bob laughed and then _____ _____.

June and Colin Gadwin

June and Colin have been married for thirteen years and they have a daughter Helen, who is nine years old.

They first met at a concert one summer, where a friend of Colin's was playing the piano in a jazz band. June knew the saxophone player in the jazz band. After the concert, the musicians and some of their friends went to a restaurant for a meal. June was sitting at the same table as Colin and they began to talk. They fell in love immediately, but Colin had a girlfriend, and June had a boyfriend. So at the end of the evening June and Colin just said goodbye.

'I thought about him every day after that evening at the restaurant, and I knew I didn't love my boyfriend Kenny,' June said. 'So a month later in July, I finished with Kenny. I didn't see Colin again until New Year's Eve. It was my birthday and the friend who plays the saxophone invited me to a party.'

> **'I thought about him every day'**

When June arrived at the house she rang the door bell and Colin opened the door. 'It was the best party I've ever been to,' said June. Later, June learned that it was Colin's idea to have the party. He asked the saxophone player to invite June because he really wanted to see her again.

Janet and Bob Rickets

Janet met Bob on an underground train in London.

Janet was sitting next to Bob when and suddenly she felt very sick. She stood up to get off at the next station. Bob looked at her and could see she was ill. He helped Janet to get off the train. But when she turned to say thank you to him, she was sick all over his shoes.

'I was really embarrassed, but he laughed,' said Janet. 'He got a taxi for me and asked me for my phone number. He said he wanted to phone and see if I was OK.'

> **'It was a really romantic evening'**

Bob phoned Janet the next day, and they went out for a meal. 'It was a really romantic evening. I promised Bob that I wouldn't be sick over him, and I wasn't. Two years later we got married.'

PRONUNCIATION

Rhyming words

8 [13.2]   Listen and circle the word on the right which rhymes with the word on the left.

1 floor	good	wood	(door)	flower
2 alone	done	only	one	phone
3 love	drove	move	glove	live
4 said	paid	made	bad	bed
5 know	now	so	new	how
6 tie	buy	toy	day	play
7 thought	cough	through	taught	enough
8 eight	height	late	what	eat

WRITING

9 Replace the underlined words with pronouns *he, she, her, them*, etc.

Jane's my best friend. (*Jane's*) (1) <u>She's</u> got black hair and (*Jane's*) (2) _____ hair is very long. (*Jane's*) (3) _____ eyes are beautiful. (*Jane's eyes*) (4) _____ are big and blue. (*Jane's*) (5) _____ very short, but (*Jane's*) (6) _____ parents are tall. (*Jane's parents*) (7) _____ are nearly two metres tall. Jane and I met when (*Jane and I*) (8) _____ were at school. Now, (*Jane*) (9) _____ is my brother's girlfriend. (*My brother*) (10) _____ wants to marry (*Jane*) (11) _____. (*My brother*) (12) _____ gave (*Jane*) (13) _____ an engagement ring last week. I gave (*Jane and my brother*) (14) _____ a book about photography for an engagement present. (*The book*) (15) _____ is a beautiful book. (*My brother and Jane*) (16) _____ want to get married next year. Then Jane won't only be my best friend, (*Jane*) (17) _____ will also be my sister-in-law.

DICTATION

Vocabulary

10 [13.3]   Read these sentences. Then listen and correct the wrong information.

1 Jane's got beautiful short, curly, red hair.
   <u>*Jane's got beautiful, long, straight, blonde hair.*</u>

2 Peter's really tall. He's got a square face, blue eyes and lovely, short, black hair.
   _____
   _____

3 I bought a really nice, short, black dress today.
   _____

4 I like that big, square, wooden box. I could keep all my love letters in it.
   _____
   _____.

5 Susan's really tidy. She always puts her clothes in the wardrobe.
   _____
   _____.

A real fan

GRAMMAR

Used to and didn't use to

1 Pam, Jan and Gillie are friends. Jan and Gillie haven't seen Pam for six months. They all meet for a meal in a restaurant.

Complete the conversation with *used to* or *didn't use to* or the Present Simple.

GILLIE: Would you like a cigarette, Pam?

PAM: No, thanks. I (*no smoke*) (1) <u>don't smoke</u> now.

JAN: But you (*smoke*) (2) <u>used to smoke</u> forty cigarettes a day!

PAM: I know I did, but I've changed a lot since January. I (*not exercise*) (3) _____ but now I (*go*) (4) _____ running every morning before work.

JAN: Do you really? I am surprised. I can remember when Gillie and I (*ask*) (5) _____ you to come swimming with us.

GILLIE: Yes. It was impossible. You (*stay*) (6) _____ at home every evening and watch TV.

PAM: Yes, but everything's different now.

GILLIE: Well, let's order. Shall we all have chicken?

PAM: I (*not eat*) (7) _____ chicken now. I'm a vegetarian.

JAN: But you always ate meat before. You (*love*) (8) _____ it.

PAM: Yes, I know. But my new boyfriend, Adam is a sports teacher and a vegetarian!

JAN: Ah. Now I understand. OK, shall we all have vegetables? And chocolate cake for dessert?

GILLIE: Oh no. Pam (*eat*) (9) _____ chocolate, but she never (*eat*) (10) _____ it now.

PAM: Yes, I do. Some things never change. I'll have four pieces of chocolate cake, please!

Past Simple or *used to*?

2 a) We cannot use *used to* + base form in four of these sentences. Which sentences aren't correct?

1 Last week I used to smoke a lot of cigarettes. **✗**
2 I didn't use to exercise, but now I exercise every day. ___
3 I bought an old car. I used to pay £50 for it. ___
4 When my daughter was a baby she didn't use to sleep very much. ___
5 We used to get our first TV when I was twelve. ___
6 I'm tired, and I used to sleep for ten hours last night. ___

b) Correct the four sentences.

_____
_____
_____
_____

Question tags

3 Match the sentences with the correct question tags.

1 Jack lives in Birmingham,   a) hasn't she?
2 John wasn't ill yesterday,   b) isn't she?
3 Peter's sold his old car,   c) doesn't he?
4 Sheila's going out tonight,   d) do they?
5 Marilyn doesn't like coffee,   e) was he?
6 Sylvia's got a car,   f) does she?
7 Tom and Ben don't like jazz,   g) hasn't he?

Time expressions

4 Correct the prepositions in these sentences if necessary. Remember some expressions do not need a preposition. Four sentences are correct.

1 I met her at the airport ~~on~~ yesterday. _✗_
2 I can come on the afternoon. ____
3 I left the office at 7 pm. ____
4 His birthday's in February. ____
5 My English class starts on 2 pm. ____
6 I go skiing at winter. ____
7 Pam's going on holiday next week. ____
8 I saw that film on TV in last month. ____
9 I'll buy a phonecard tomorrow. ____

VOCABULARY

Entertainment

5 Look at the pictures and complete the sentences.

1 I need some new  _batteries_ for my
  ____.

2 If you go to Japan, will you get me a
   ____?

3 That's a terrible noise. Please, use your
   ____.

4 Have you got a  ____?

5 Have you got this on  ____?

6 I haven't got a  ____ player.

6 Complete the paragraph with one of the words from the box.

> theatre acting booked clapped stage
> audience interval front row programme
> performance

I went to the (1) _theatre_ last night. It was awful. I
(2) _____ my seat weeks ago, and I was very
excited about going. I paid a lot of money to get a
(3) _____ seat. When I arrived I bought a
(4) _____ which was £5. I thought that was
very expensive. The (5) _____ was bad. One
actor fell off the (6) _____! Only a few people
(7) _____ and most of the (8) _____ left at
the (9) _____ and didn't stay to see the second
half of the (10) _____.

7 a) Match the names of instruments with the pictures.

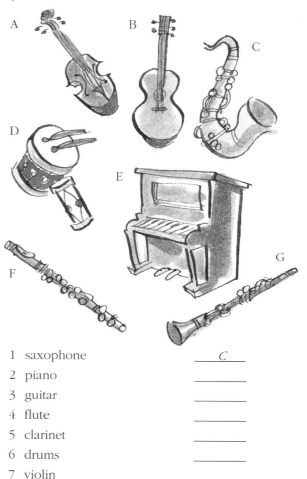

1 saxophone   _C_
2 piano   _____
3 guitar   _____
4 flute   _____
5 clarinet   _____
6 drums   _____
7 violin   _____

b) [📼 14.1] Listen and mark the stressed
syllable in each word.

LISTENING

8 a) Before you listen, think about these questions.

1 What do you do in your free time?
2 What do you like doing most?

b) We interviewed three people in the street. We asked them 'What is your idea of a good evening's entertainment?'
[🔲 14.2] Listen to Marc, Carol and Sally. Who talks about:

1 films? _____
2 books? _____
3 music? _____
4 art galleries? _____

c) Listen again. Put a ✔ next to the information you hear.

1 Marc is a musician. ✔
2 Marc plays the guitar. ___
3 Marc is in a group that plays rock and reggae music. ___
4 Marc goes to the theatre twice a week. ___
5 Marc earns a lot of money as a musician. ___
6 Carol is a writer. ___
7 Carol often goes out in the evening. ___
8 Carol likes classical music. __
9 Carol enjoys staying at home and reading. ___
10 Sally doesn't work. ___
11 Sally likes art galleries. ___
12 There aren't many free art galleries. ___
13 Sally hasn't got much money. ___
14 Sally doesn't have a video recorder. ___

54

WRITING

Adverbs

9 A director is talking to the actors in his new film. Replace the adjectives in brackets with adverbs.

Oh, I can see Harrison's late again! OK everyone. Today I want you to speak (*clear*) (1) *clearly*. Yesterday's filming was awful! James, I want you to walk to the hotel (*quick*) (2) _____. You walked so (*slow*) (3) _____ yesterday I fell asleep waiting for you. Remember, you're going to kill Sarah. So you walk across the road (*quick*) (4) _____ and (*angry*) (5) _____. Sarah, you did the dying scene (*very good*) (6) _____ yesterday but you died before James shot you! Today, please, listen more (*careful*) (7) _____ to the other actors. Simon, you spoke so (*quiet*) (8) _____ yesterday that I didn't hear a word you said. Ah, Harrison. You're here, finally! We're all waiting (*patient*) (9) _____ to begin.

DICTATION

Sound and spelling: *a*

10 a) [🔲 14.3] Listen and complete the sentences.

1 _____ do you _____ from the _____?
2 I have to go now. But on _____ I can _____ to you _____ day.
3 I can't _____. I'll have to _____ if I miss my _____.
4 I'm _____ that you _____ your _____.
5 John's very _____. He was first in the _____, but I was _____.

b) All the missing words have the letter *a* in them. In each sentence, two of the three missing words have the same pronunciation of *a*. Listen again and circle the two words.

11 [🔲 14.4] Listen to the words in the box. Write them in the correct place in the table.

| what fat train all park want bank Saturday made |
| fall sad talk wall late bad exam car fan ball |

/ɒ/	/æ/	/eɪ/	/ɔː/	/ɑː/
wh*a*t	f*a*t	tr*ai*n	*a*ll	p*a*rk

School rules

GRAMMAR

Someone, anyone, no one, everyone, something, anything, nothing and everything

1 Read these letters from two teenagers at a boarding school. Circle the correct word.

Dear Mum and Dad,

I hate this boarding school! I've been here for a day, but I haven't met (1) someone/(anyone) like yet. I'm really bored because there's (2) something/nothing to do in the evenings. I'm also very lonely. (3) Someone/ No one ever speaks to me. (4) Someone/Everyone is unfriendly. I want to come home.

Your unhappy son, Karl

Dear Mum and Dad,

It's a great school and I'm really happy here! I like the people a lot, (5) someone/no one is unfriendly. Yesterday (6) someone/anyone invited me to a party next Friday. I'm so busy – I'm having a great time. There is (7) something/nothing different on every evening. Tonight (8) someone/anyone is coming to teach us modern dancing. I haven't met (9) someone/anyone who doesn't like being here. No, that's wrong. There's a really unfriendly boy who hasn't spoken to (10) someone/anyone since he arrived here yesterday. It's very sad to see him so unhappy. Perhaps I'll ask him to the party then he can meet (11) anyone/everyone. (12) Everything/ Anything here is wonderful. I'll see you in the holidays.

Love Hannah

Too much or too many?

2 Complete these sentences with *too much* or *too many*.

1 I'm leaving. There are <u>*too many*</u> people here.
2 Sally ate _____ food at lunch, and she feels sick.
3 You drink _____ coffee.
4 There are _____ chairs in here. Can you take some out, please?
5 I can't come out tonight. I've got _____ homework.
6 You've got _____ pairs of shoes! You can't have any more!
7 You're making _____ noise. Please be quiet.

Correct the mistakes

3 Correct the underlined mistakes in these sentences.

1 I bought too ~~many~~ *much* milk. There's <u>any</u> _____ in the fridge.
2 A: I don't know <u>someone</u> _____ at this party.
   B: Don't worry. I know <u>anyone</u> _____ . I'll introduce you to them all.
3 <u>Anyone</u> _____ has broken my favourite cup!
4 No letters again! <u>Anyone</u> _____ has written to me for a month!
5 I'm bored. I've got <u>anything</u> _____ to do.
6 Come here a minute. I've got <u>anything</u> _____ to tell you.
7 I can't study here. There's too <u>many</u> _____ noise!
8 There are too <u>much</u> _____ people in our class. They should move <u>anyone</u> _____ to another class.

VOCABULARY

4 John and Helen are studying for their exams.

a) Complete their conversation with one of the words in the box.

> study   take (x2)   attend   fail   do   pass
> go   get

1 JOHN: Come on let's *take* a break.

2 HELEN: No. If I want to _____ the exam tomorrow, I'll have to _____ all night.

3 JOHN: This is because you didn't _____ your homework during the year.

4 HELEN: I know! I know! And I didn't _____ classes every day. I really don't know enough for the exams. I'm sure I'm going to _____ all of them.

5 JOHN: Don't say that. You're very clever. I'm sure you'll _____ all the exams, _____ to university and _____ a degree. So, come on and take a break.

6 HELEN: OK. I'll come if you help me with my maths.

JOHN: Oh, no! It isn't the maths exam tomorrow, is it? I thought it was next Monday!

HELEN: No. It's tomorrow.

JOHN: Oh! Help!

b) [📼 15.1] Listen and check your answers.

British English and American English

5 Sometimes American English has different words for things.

a) Match the English word with the American word. Use a dictionary if necessary.

English	American
1 public school	a) gas(oline)
2 state school	b) purse
3 trousers	c) public school
4 chemist's	d) private school
5 petrol	e) pants
6 handbag	f) pharmacy/drug store
7 lift	g) wallet
8 purse	h) elevator

b) [📼 15.2] Cover Exercise 5a) with a piece of paper. Read and listen to an English woman's story. Then replace the underlined words with American words.

I had a really bad day yesterday! I needed some new trousers (1) *pants* for my son who goes to public school (2) _____. I also had to get some medicine from the chemist's (3) _____, so I went there first. I bought the medicine but I left my handbag (4) _____ in the chemist's (5)_____. I got in the car and saw that I needed some petrol (6) _____ so I drove to the petrol station (7) _____ and filled up the car. When I went to pay for the petrol (8) _____ I couldn't find my handbag (9) _____ or my purse (10) _____ so I couldn't pay. I was very embarrassed and I didn't get the trousers (11) _____.

c) [📼 15.3] Listen to an American woman telling the same story and check your answers.

READING

First day at school

6 a) Before you read, think about these questions.

1 Can you remember your first day at school?
2 Did your mother take you to school?
3 Did you cry on your first day?
4 Did you enjoy your first day?

b) Read about Gillian Core's first day at school. Then look at the pictures. Put them in the correct order. *D*_____

I can remember my first day at school very well. All the new children went into the classroom with their mothers and then the teacher told the mothers to leave. Most of the children started to cry. I didn't cry because I wanted to be a 'big' girl and go to school like my older sister and brother. After the mothers left, the teacher said, 'Now children, stand up, put your hands together, close your eyes and we'll say a prayer.'

I stood up. I put my hands together and I said the prayer. But I was four and a half years old, I was excited and I didn't want to close my eyes. I wanted to look at everything and everyone in the room.

When the prayer was finished, the teacher told me to go to the front of the class. Then she started shouting, 'This naughty girl did not close her eyes like everyone else when we said the prayer.'

By this time the other children had stopped crying, and that's when I began to cry. The teacher made me stand in the corner of the room until playtime. While I was standing in the corner I was thinking, 'If the teacher could see that my eyes were open, her eyes were open, too. So why isn't she standing in the corner?'

After that I didn't want to be 'big' like my brother and sister. I didn't want to go to school ever again!

c) Read the story again and answer these questions.

1 Did Gillian want to go to school? *Yes, she did*.
2 Did she cry when her mother left? _____.
3 Did she enjoy her first day? _____.
4 Did she want to go to school on the second day? _____.

d) Complete these sentences.

1 Gillian didn't cry at the beginning because *she wanted to go to school.*
2 The other children cried because _____ _____.
3 After the mothers left, the teacher told the children to _____.
4 The teacher shouted at Gillian because _____ _____.
5 Gillian cried because _____ _____.

WRITING

Linking words

7 Use one of the linking words in the box to complete the sentences.

and   but   so   because   although   however
also

1 Jack __*and*__ Jim go to the same school.
2 _____ it was raining, we went for a walk.
3 James goes to public school. Penny _____ goes to public school.
4 I wanted to go to the school dance _____ I had to look after my sister at home.
5 I couldn't go to the school dance _____ I had to look after my sister at home.
6 I didn't do any studying _____ I failed my exam.
7 I didn't do any studying. _____, I passed my exam.

DICTATION

Vocabulary and word stress

8 [🔲 15.4]   Listen and complete the sentences.

1 I _____.
2 John _____.
3 I _____.
4 Jennifer's _____.

9 [🔲 15.5]   Listen. Write the words you hear and mark the stressed syllable.

1 *'politics*	2 _____	3 _____
4 _____	5 _____	6 _____
7 _____	8 _____	9 _____

Have you heard the news?

GRAMMAR

Passives

1 Complete these sentences with *is/are/was/were made of/in*.

1 Volkswagen cars _are made in_ Germany.

2 The jacket _is made of_ cotton.

3 Alfa Romeo cars _____ Italy.

4 The table _____ wood and glass.

5 Moët et Chandon champagne _____ France.

6 These bags _____ the very best English leather.

7 The hand painted boxes _____ Hungary.

8 This furniture _____ 1901.

9 My jewellery box is very old. It _____ the last century.

2 Read the article about the cinema and underline all the Past Simple and Past Simple Passive forms. There are seven Past Simple Passive forms and seven Past Simple forms. Then complete the box

THE HISTORY OF CINEMA

An American, Thomas Edison, <u>made</u> the first machine with moving pictures in 1891. It <u>was called</u> a kinetoscope. Then in 1895 a machine that projected pictures on to a screen was built by two French brothers, Auguste and Louis Lumière. They called their machine a *cinematographe*. The pictures from this machine were shown one after the other very quickly.

The Lumière brothers gave the world's first public film show in 1896, and in America the world's first cinema was built in Pittsburgh in 1905.

In the beginning films were made to show news, but by 1902 filmmakers began to write stories for film and use actors. These films were very popular in America, and Hollywood became important in the film making industry. The first 'talkie' (film and sound) was shown in America in 1927. It was called *The Jazz Singer*.

Past Simple	Past Simple Passive
1 *made*	1 *was called*
2	2
3	3
4	4
5	5
6	6
7	7

3 Correct the verb form mistakes in these questions.

1 Who was made the kinetoscope?

　A: _Who made the kinetoscope?_

　B: Thomas Edison.

2 Who was built the *cinematographe*?

　A: _____?

　B: The Lumière brothers.

3 What the machine called?

　A: _____?

　B: It was called a *cinematographe*.

4 When the world's first public film was shown?

　A: _____?

　B: In 1896 in Paris.

5 Where the first cinema built?

　A: _____?

　B: In Pittsburgh, in the USA.

6 When the first talkie was made?

　A: _____?

　B: In 1927.

7 When filmmakers begin to use actors?

　A: _____?

　B: In 1902.

4 Read about the Halton hotel and make sentences using the Present Simple Passive.

1 We change the beds every day.
   The beds are changed every day.

2 We wash the towels every day.
   The towels _____.

3 We clean the rooms every day.
   The rooms _____.

4 We only use fresh food.
   Only fresh food _____.

5 We bring breakfast to your room.
   Breakfast _____.

6 We give our customers the best service.
   Our customers _____.

VOCABULARY

Negatives

5 Make the words in the box negative. Use *dis-*, *un-* and *in-*. Then complete these sentences.

| kind lucky satisfied tidy agree happy |
| experienced correct |

1 I never walk under a ladder. I think it's *unlucky*.

2 Do you really think that picture's good? I
   _____. I think it's awful!

3 What's the matter? You look very _____.

4 This answer is _____.

5 Why did you shout at that old man? That was
   _____.

6 Your room looks terrible! It's very _____.

7 That journalist only started working last week.
   He's very _____.

8 I want to talk to the manager of the hotel,
   immediately. I was very _____ with my room
   and the service!

Words and spelling

6 [🔲 16.1]   Some words have the same sounds but different spellings and different meanings. Listen to these sounds. Then write the correct word in the sentences.

1 /baɪ/   bye/buy
   a) Elizabeth's not here. She's gone to *buy*
      some coffee.
   b) Where's Liam? I want to say good*bye* to him.

2 /peə/   pair/pear
   a) I'm hungry. Can I have a _____, please?
   b) I need a new _____ of socks.

3 /rəʊd/   road/rode
   a) Peter _____ his bicycle to work yesterday.
   b) Do you live on the King's _____?

4 /ðeə/   their/there
   a) Can you put the books _____, please?
   b) This is _____ house.

5 /wʌn/   one/won
   a) I need a pen. Have you got _____?
   b) Who _____ the football match yesterday?

6 /nəʊz/   knows/nose
   a) I really don't like my _____!
   b) Ask Pam. She _____ the answer.

LISTENING

A

B

C

7 a) [🔲 16.2]   Listen to the news. Match the pictures with the stories.

1 The first story   = picture _____

2 The second story = picture _____

3 The third story   = picture _____

b) Answer these questions with short answers.

The first story

1 Were the two boys brothers? _Yes, they were_ .

2 Were the boys playing in their bedroom? _____.

3 Did Mrs Dayton see the smoke? _____.

4 Were the boys taken to hospital? _____.

5 Were the boys badly injured? _____.

The second story

6 Was Janice playing near a swimming pool? _____.

7 Did her ball fall into the river? _____.

8 Did Janice's dog push her into the water? _____.

9 Was she saved by the dog? _____.

10 Was her mother taken to hospital? _____.

11 Was Janice injured? _____.

The third story

12 Is this the first time the beach has been closed? _____.

13 Did the police tell people not to go into the sea? _____.

14 Did the jellyfish sting anyone? _____.

15 Were people taken to hospital? _____.

WRITING

Punctuation

8 Punctuate this newspaper article. Use full stops (**.**), commas (**,**), capital letters (**America**), speech marks (' ') and apostrophes (**I'm**).

1 yesterday afternoon a bank in the centre of london was robbed

Yesterday afternoon a bank in the centre of London was robbed.

2 two men wearing black leather coats ran into the bank with guns

_____

_____

3 the bank manager said the two men shouted at us all and told us all to sit on the floor with our hands on our heads

_____

_____

_____

4 the two men put £30000 into a red suitcase and ran out of the building

_____

_____

5 however the suitcase wasnt closed properly so all the money fell out onto the street

_____

_____

_____

6 the two men were caught while they were trying to pick the money up

_____

_____

_____

DICTATION

Passives

9 [🔊 16.3]   The information in these sentences is incorrect. Listen and write the sentences correctly.

1 President Abraham Lincoln was killed by a soldier.

_____.

2 The telephone was invented by A. G. Bell in 1874.

_____.

3 Paper was invented by the Japanese.

_____.

4 Photography was invented in the 1890s.

_____.

5 The Statue of Liberty was given to the American people by the British government.

_____

_____.

6 The Taj Mahal in India was built by Shah Jahan for his favourite daughter who died in 1631.

_____

_____

_____.

Celebration!

GRAMMAR

Present Perfect Simple and Continuous

1 Complete these sentences with *for* or *since*.

1 I've known him <u>since</u> last April.
2 Sam's been watching TV _____ he got up this morning.
3 Jacky's lived in Athens _____ six years.
4 Liz's been waiting _____ an hour.
5 I've been ill _____ Monday.
6 We've been married _____ two months.
7 I've known Marilyn _____ 1992.
8 I haven't had any letters _____ last week.
9 He hasn't known Mary _____ very long.
10 This isn't new. I've had it _____ years.

2 Put these words in the correct order to make questions. The first word is given.

1 How/talking/long/has/the/on/phone/he/been
   <u>How long has he been talking on the phone</u>?
2 Has/working/been/he/Christmas/since/here
   _____?
3 Have/they/their/car/long/had/for
   _____?
4 How/known/you/long/have/Peter
   _____?
5 Who/eating/chocolate/has/been/my
   _____?
6 How/has/that/new/long/Mary/had/sports/car
   _____?
7 Have/been/waiting/you/for/us/long/for
   _____?
8 Have/seen/my/you/key/car
   _____?

3 Tim, Ben and John are university students. They live in the same flat. Complete this conversation with the Present Perfect Simple or the Present Perfect Continuous.

BEN: Where's John?
TIM: He's asleep.
BEN: He's still sleeping! He's been (*sleep*) (1) <u>sleeping</u> all day.
TIM: Leave him. He's (*be*) (2) _____ ill.
BEN: Ill! You mean he's (*have*) (3) _____ a cold for two days. That's nothing.
TIM: It's not just a cold. He hasn't (*be*) (4) _____ well since his girlfriend left him.
BEN: Look! I've (*know*) (5) _____ John a lot longer than you have. He's really lazy. He knows Saturday is house cleaning day. That's why he's in bed.
TIM: Oh, don't wake him up. I've been (*do*) (6) _____ the housework all afternoon. I've nearly (*finish*) (7) _____.
BEN: Do you know, he hasn't (*wash*) (8) _____ a cup since he moved in last year. Nothing!
TIM: He needs our help, Ben. Be nice. He hasn't got any money, so he can't move out.
BEN: He never has any money. He's been (*borrow*) (9) _____ money from me for months.
TIM: Has he? He's been (*borrow*) (10) _____ money from me, too!
BEN: I've (*give*) (11) _____ him £40 this week.
TIM: Me too! OK, let's wake him.
BEN: But, Tim, he hasn't (*be*) (12) _____ well.
TIM: I don't care! I want my money back!

4 Complete these sentences with Present Perfect Continuous or Present Perfect Simple. Use the verbs in the brackets.

1 (*walk*) He *'s been walking* for two hours.
1 (*walk*) He _____ eight miles.
3 (*read*) I _____ three hundred pages.
4 (*read*) I _____ all morning.
5 (*write*) She _____ letters all week.
6 (*write*) She _____ ten letters this morning.

VOCABULARY

5 Circle the correct word.

1 He's studying *photographer*/*photography*.
2 Simone took this picture. She's a really good *photographer/photograph*.
3 She's an *electric/electrical* engineer.
4 Don't keep her waiting. She's not a very *patient/patience* person.
5 I have to make a *decide/decision* before tomorrow.
6 You can *choose/choice* the wine tonight.
7 I need a *medicine/medical* dictionary.
8 Look at those flowers. They're *dead/died*.
9 Pauline is *married/marriage* to Clive.
10 There has been a *robber/robbery* at the bank!

6 Complete this table to make word families.

	Adjective	Adverb	Noun	Verb
1	interested			–
2		safely		–
3		–	friend	–
4	–	–		rob
5	happy			–
6	worried			
7	photographic			

LISTENING

7 **a)** Before you listen, think about a festival in your country.

1 Do you have special food?
2 Do all the people in your family have dinner together?
3 Do you give presents to people?

b) [🔊 17.1]   Listen to Jeff talking about Christmas and answer these questions. Use short answers.

1 Did Jeff enjoy Christmas Day when he was a child? *No, he didn't.*
2 Does he enjoy Christmas now?_____.
3 Is he going to have Christmas with his family this year? _____.

c) Listen again. Are these sentences *True* (T) or *False* (F)?

1 Jeff thinks most people like Christmas. _*F*_
2 When he was a child, Jeff liked his presents. _____
3 When he was a child, Christmas was always a quiet day at home with the family. _____
4 There were always terrible family arguments on Christmas Day. _____
5 These days Jeff doesn't usually have Christmas with his family. _____

d) Listen again and answer these questions.

1 Jeff tells us three things his family argued about. What are they? _____
2 Why did everyone feel sick on Christmas Day?
_____
3 Jeff thinks that people in shops aren't very nice at Christmas. What three things does he say about them? _____
4 What present does Aunt Lucy buy Jeff every year?_____
5 Why is this not a good present for Jeff?
_____
6 What is Jeff going to do on Christmas Day this year?_____

WRITING

Paragraphs

8 Read this letter and put a line where you think a new paragraph should begin. There are four paragraphs. The first one finishes after *handwriting*.

28 Sumner Rd
Keithly
Jan 3rd

Dear Auntie June,

Thank you for the <u>nice</u> fountain pen. I've always wanted one like this. It really is <u>nice</u> and it certainly helps my handwriting. │ I hope you had a <u>nice</u> time at Christmas. I stayed with some <u>nice</u> friends and we had a <u>nice</u> time. I ate a lot of <u>nice</u> food and I'm kilos heavier now which is <u>not very nice</u>. I'm going on a diet this afternoon! University starts again next week. I'm taking some very <u>nice</u> courses. I really like the photography course, it's very <u>nice</u>. However, the chemistry course is <u>not nice</u>. I hate it! I have to go into town to buy some books that I need for next term, so I have to finish this letter now. Thank you again for the <u>nice</u> pen, and I hope you have a <u>nice</u> New Year.

Best wishes
Jonathan

Improving the letter

9 a) Look at the adjectives in the box. Which are positive and which are negative? Make two lists.

awful   wonderful   interesting   bad   brilliant
dreadful   lovely   fantastic   great   terrible
excellent   good   delicious

b) On a separate piece of paper, rewrite Jonathan's letter with four paragraphs. Replace the underlined words with adjectives from your lists.

DICTATION

Contrastive stress

10 a) [🔲 17.2]   Listen and write what B says.

1 A: The bus leaves at eight o'clock.
   B: _____.

2 A: Did you ask for coffee?
   B: _____.

3 A: John bought a blue and white striped jumper.
   B: _____.

4 A: We're going to New York today.
   B: _____.

b) Listen again. Mark the main stressed syllable in each sentence.

1 A: The bus leaves at 'eight o'clock.

Love your neighbour

GRAMMAR

Sentence patterns and reported sentences

1 Rewrite the sentences using *asked me* or *told me*.

1 'Please bring me some water.'
She asked me to bring her some water.

2 'Please don't make any noise after 11 pm.'
He (*ask*) _____.

3 'Don't tell anyone.'
They (*tell*) _____.

4 'Can you open the window, please?'
She (*ask*) _____.

5 'You must stop work.'
Tom (*tell*) _____.

6 'Could you drive Steve to the party?'
Sylvia (*ask*) _____.

7 'Please don't smoke in this room.'
They (*ask*) _____.

8 'Come back again in an hour.'
Francis (*tell*) _____.

9 'Don't give Nicholas anything to drink.'
The doctor (*tell*) _____.

2 a) [📼 18.1]   It's Monday morning in the office. David and Maggie are talking. Read and listen to their conversation.

DAVID: Jim wants to leave.

MAGGIE: I know he's very unhappy here.

DAVID: Mmm. He really doesn't like his manager.

MAGGIE: That's because his manager is a woman.

DAVID: He's going to apply for a job in America.

MAGGIE: There are more women managers in America than in England.

DAVID: Mmm. Don't tell Jim!

b) It's lunchtime. Maggie is telling her friend about her conversation with David. Complete the reported sentences in the past.

1 David told *me Jim wanted to leave*.

2 I said _____.

3 Then David said Jim _____.

4 I told _____.

5 Then David told _____.

6 I said _____.

7 Then David told _____.

c) [📼 18.2]   Listen and check your answers.

3 Put a cross next to the incorrect sentences. Correct the mistakes.

1 He told me go home immediately. **✗**
He told me to go home immediately.

2 I wanted to go to the cinema, but I didn't have enough money. ___
_____

3 I'd like to visit my brother in Holland next week. ___
_____

4 I wanted buy you some flowers, but I couldn't find any. ___
_____

5 He asked to use the phone, and I said yes. ___
_____

6 He decided not change his job. ___
_____

7 I want ask you a question. ___
_____

8 She promised to get up early. ___

_____

9 James told Helen not to send the letter before
   next week. ___

_____

10 I enjoyed watching tennis. ___

_____

11 He said me Jane was ill. ___

_____

12 I finished to work at seven o'clock last night.

   ___

_____

VOCABULARY

Phrasal verbs

4 a) Match the phrasal verbs with their meanings.

1 turn up	a)	escape
2 give up	b)	wait for a short time
3 break down	c)	arrive
4 take off	d)	visit someone at their home
5 run away	e)	leave
6 bring back	f)	remove
7 go away	g)	stop
8 hold on	h)	stop working
9 come round	i)	return something
10 come over	j)	walk towards someone

b) Replace the underlined words with the correct
form of one phrasal verb.

LYNNE: Mary told me you had a terrible experience
        on your way home last night.
JUNE: Yes, I did. I was driving home when the car
        stopped working (1) _broke down_. A man
        stopped and walked towards my car.
LYNNE: To help?
JUNE: Well, it was dark and I was very frightened.
        So, I decided to escape (2) _____. I heard
        him shout, 'Wait, (3) _____ I want to help.'
LYNNE: Then what happened?
JUNE: I had some money in my pocket so I got a
        bus home. But that's not the end of the
        story. I got home and removed (4) _____
        my coat. Then the man arrived
        (5) _____ at the door.
LYNNE: No!
JUNE: Yes, he did. But he only wanted to bring me
        my car keys and my handbag. He was a very
        nice person. He saw my keys and my bag in
        the car and the doors were open. He didn't
        want anyone to steal my car or my bag.

LYNNE: Oh, how nice of him.
JUNE: Yes, it was.
LYNNE: Oh, look at the time. Are you playing
        tennis tonight?
JUNE: No. I've stopped (6) _____ playing tennis.
        I'm no good at it. But why don't you visit
        me (7) _____ after your game?
LYNNE: Yes, thanks. I will. See you about eight,
        and I'll return (8) _____ the video I
        borrowed from you.

c) [▭ 18.3]   Listen and check your answers.

Do or *make*?

5 Complete the sentences with *do* or *make*.

1 Look. I didn't _make_ any mistakes in my
   homework!
2 I'm sorry the house is untidy. I didn't _____
   any housework today.
3 You look tired. I'll _____ the washing up for
   you.
4 Will you _____ me a cup of coffee, please?
5 Please, don't _____ a noise. Beth's asleep.
6 Come round for dinner tonight, and I'll
   _____ a pizza.

READING

6 a) [📼 18.4]   Read this story. Then listen to the cassette.

Betty watched her new, good-looking neighbour every day. She watched him leave the house every morning. She watched him come home from work every evening. She took photos of his friends when they visited him. She took photos of him in his garden. She watched him all the time, but he didn't know.

One Saturday morning he left his house at ten o'clock, and Betty decided to follow him. He did his shopping and then went into a video shop and got two videos. After that he began to walk up the road back to his house. Betty passed him and arrived at her house a few minutes before him. She waited for him to turn the corner and then she bumped into him. He dropped his shopping bag and the food fell onto the road.

'Oh, I'm very, very sorry,' said Betty. 'Please let me help you.'

'Don't worry,' said the young man. 'I can manage.'

'No, really, I feel terrible. All your food is on the road. You can't eat it now,' said Betty.

Betty introduced herself, and told him she was his neighbour. Then she asked him to come round for dinner at her house that evening. 'I've got lots of food. I'd really like to cook for you,' she said. 'I feel so bad about this.' Betty wanted the young man to accept her offer, but he did not.

'OK, but I want to pay for the food,' explained Betty, but again he said no.

Although he didn't want any help, Betty carried some of the shopping to his front door. She wanted him to invite her inside, but he didn't. He just said, 'Thank you, and don't worry. I'll get a hamburger later.'

Betty was very angry that her plan hadn't worked, and she went to her usual place by the window and started watching him again.

b) What do you think?

1 Is Betty beautiful or not?
2 How old is the young man?
3 How old is Betty?
4 Do you think this is the beginning of a love story?
5 Do you think this is the beginning of a murder story?

c) Listen to the Dictation to find the answers.

DICTATION

7 [📼 18.5]   Listen and complete the sentences.

1 Betty was tall and slim, _____.

2 Betty _____.

3 The young man _____.

4 It's _____.

WRITING

Stories

8 Finish the story about Betty. These questions will help you to think of ideas.

1 Who is dead, Betty or the young man?
2 Who is the murderer, Betty, the young man or another person?
3 Why did the murderer do it?
4 How did the murderer kill the person who is dead?

This is the last line of the story. Choose the people to fit your murder mystery.

The body of Betty/the young man was never found, and everything was quiet in the street until the following year when another woman/young man moved into the house next door!

_____

_____

_____

_____

_____

_____

_____

_____

_____

PRONUNCIATION

Sound and spelling: *u*

9 [18.5] We can pronounce the letter *u* in different ways. Listen to the words in the box and write them in the correct place.

untidy pull purse blue united under must full nurse uniform usual cup church button umbrella put lunch hurt unhappy university

/ʌ/	/ʊ/	/ɜː/	/uː/	/juː/
untidy	*pull*	*purse*	*blue*	*united*

Team spirit

GRAMMAR

If or *unless*?

1 Choose a) or b) to complete the sentences.

1 We'll stay at home ...
   a) *if it rains.* ✓
   b) unless it rains. ✗

2 We'll go for a long walk ...
   a) if it rains. ___
   b) unless it rains. ___

3 I'll give you £5 ...
   a) if I have enough money. ___
   b) unless I have enough money. ___

4 We'll eat about eight ...
   a) if you're hungry now. ___
   b) unless you're hungry now. ___

5 I'll drive you to school ...
   a) if you want to walk. ___
   b) unless you want to walk. ___

6 We won't be late ...
   a) if we leave now. ___
   b) unless we leave now. ___

7 I'll buy you that book ...
   a) if you like it. ___
   b) unless you like it. ___

8 I'll take a taxi to the airport ...
   a) if there's a bus. ___
   b) unless there's a bus. ___

9 Jeffrey will fail his exams ...
   a) if he studies harder. ___
   b) unless he studies harder. ___

10 Andy will love the party ...
   a) if he comes. ___
   b) unless he comes. ___

Verb patterns 1

if/when/unless/as soon as	+ present verb form

will	+ base form of the verb

2 Put the verb in the correct form.

LENNY: Bruce, is everything ready for the party?

BRUCE: No. Nothing!!

LENNY: Unless you (*hurry up*) (1) *hurry up*, everyone (*be*) (2) _____ here.

BRUCE: I know that! I'm not stupid. If you (*look*) (3) _____ around, you (*see*) (4) _____ the problem.

LENNY: Oh! What happened?

BRUCE: There was a fire in the kitchen.

LENNY: How did it happen?

BRUCE: I was cooking some chicken for the party, when the pan caught fire! Look at the mess! I phoned James a few minutes ago and he's coming to help. We must clean the place.

LENNY: I (*start*) (5) _____ cleaning now if you (*want*) (6) _____. And when James (*arrive*) (7) _____, I (*go*) (8) _____ to the supermarket for some food.

BRUCE: Thank you, Lenny, but I don't think I've got any more cash. I'll look in my jacket pocket.

LENNY: Don't worry. If you (*not have got*)
(9) _____ any, I (*buy*) (10) _____ the
food.

BRUCE: You're a good friend, Lenny, thanks. I
(*give*) (11) _____ you the money back
as soon as the bank (*open*) (12) _____
on Monday.

LENNY: OK. Let's start cleaning.

Verb patterns 2

3 Put these words in the correct order. The first
word of the sentence is given.

1 I my friend sent a present
   I sent my friend a present.

2 I my friend to sent a present
   I sent a present to my friend.

3 Jim brought flowers Rebecca some

   _____.

4 Sam read son his to a story

   _____.

5 We take will tea some Mary

   _____.

6 Please take Mary it to

   _____.

7 Please show this James picture

   _____.

8 I gave to John bag the

   _____.

9 Can me pass you the salt please

   _____?

VOCABULARY

Spelling

4 a) These letters are in the wrong order. Put
them in the right order to make words connected
with sport.

1 actmh   _match_
2 otbfaoll   _____
3 tbae   _____
4 rseocu   _____
5 ckart   _____
6 loga   _____
7 kctera   _____
8 rctuo   _____
9 wrtoh   _____

b) Use one of the words in the box to complete
the sentences.

> boxing   catch   kick   scored   match   went
> basketball   golf

1 Are you going to watch the tennis _match_ on
   TV?

2 Italy _____ three goals in fifteen minutes.

3 Gillian _____ jogging for the first time
   yesterday.

4 Do you know how to play _____?

5 Do you always _____ the ball with your left
   foot?

6 Quick! _____ the ball!

7 Alan's at the _____ club.

8 I bought my wife some _____ gloves for her
   birthday.

LISTENING

5 a) Have you ever had an accident while you were playing sports?

b) Match the pictures with the words.

1 to fit ____   5 advanced slope ____
2 to hire ____   6 skis ____
3 nursery slope ____   7 ski poles ____
4 blood (noun), to bleed (verb) ____

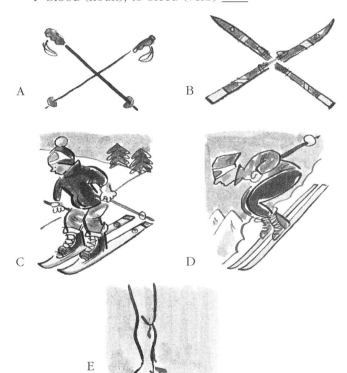

6 [🔊 19.1]   Annie is talking about an accident. Listen and look at the pictures. Which picture is **not** from the story? ____

a) Listen again and complete these sentences.

1 When Annie was living in Canada her friends said she should learn _to ski._

2 The only part of the day that she enjoyed was the _____.

3 Annie couldn't ski but her friends were _____ skiers.

4 Annie's friends left her on the 'nursery' slope which was where all the _____ were skiing.

5 One of the children skied into Annie's _____.

6 Annie wasn't worried about herself, but she was worried about the little _____.

7 There was some _____ in the snow, but the little girl wasn't _____.

8 The blood in the snow was from Annie's _____.

9 Annie was in _____ for a week.

WRITING

Punctuation

7 These sentences are from the beginning of a short story. Use speech marks (' '), commas (,), apostrophes ('), full stops (.) and capital letters (**America**) to punctuate them.

1 mrs evans walked into the living room where her husband was watching tv

_____

_____

2 not another football match she said thats the third today

_____

_____

3 mr evans told his wife to be quiet

_____

_____

4 you dont need to listen to a football match said mrs evans

_____

_____

5 OK but i dont want to listen to you said her husband

_____

_____

6 mrs evans went to the kitchen and took a large knife from the drawer

_____

_____

DICTATION

Rhythm and sentence stress

8 a)[🔲 19.2]   Listen and write the sentences.

1 _Where did she go?_

2 _____?

3 _____?

4 _____?

5 _____?

6 _____?

7 _____?

8 _____?

b) Listen again. Which sentence stress pattern is used? There is a symbol for each word in the sentence. The most important stressed word is ■ and the other stressed words are ●.

1 a) ● o o ■ ✓   b) o ■ o o ✗

2 a) ● o o ■ ___   b) o o ■ o ___

3 a) ● o o ■ ___   b) o o ● ■ ___

4 a) ● o ■ ___   b) o o ■ ___

5 a) ● o o ■ o o ___   b) o o ● ● o ■ ___

6 a) ● o ■ o ___   b) o o ■ o ___

7 a) o o ■ o ___   b) ■ o o o ___

8 a) o o ● ■ o ___   b) ● o o o ■ ___

Going away

GRAMMAR

Revision of Units 11–19

1 Correct the underlined mistakes in these two sentences.

1 Your bike is <u>more good</u> than mine. (Unit 11)
  Your bike is better than mine.

2 My sister isn't as <u>taller</u> as me. (Unit 11)
  _____.

3 If I had more time, I <u>go</u> to the cinema more often. (Unit 12)
  _____.

4 If I <u>don't</u> smoke, I'd have more money. (Unit 12)
  _____.

5 It's a <u>leather brown big</u> bag. (Unit 13)
  _____.

6 There's the shop <u>that</u> I bought my book. (Unit 13)
  _____.

7 Yesterday I <u>used to go</u> to the shop. (Unit 14)
  _____.

8 He works here, <u>isn't</u> he? (Unit 14)
  _____.

9 There's <u>anyone</u> at the door. (Unit 15)
  _____.

10 There's too <u>many</u> sugar in my tea. (Unit 15)
  _____.

11 The murderer was <u>take</u> to prison. (Unit 16)
  _____.

12 They <u>was</u> given two free tickets for the theatre. (Unit 16)
  _____.

13 I've <u>been knowing</u> John for ten years. (Unit 17)
  _____.

14 I've been learning English <u>since</u> two years. (Unit 17)
  _____.

15 He asked me <u>going</u> to his office at 10 am. (Unit 18)
  _____.

16 <u>If</u> we clean up our mess, Mum will be angry. (Unit 19)
  _____.

17 I gave <u>to John</u> the money for the tickets. (Unit 19)
  _____.

18 As soon as <u>she'll arrive</u>, we'll call for a taxi. (Unit 19)
  _____.

Comparatives

2 a) Rewrite these sentences with the adjectives in brackets using the comparative. The meaning must stay the same.

1 Last year's course wasn't as good as this year's.
  (*good*) *This year's course is better than last year's* .

2 This hotel isn't as expensive as the Hilton.
  (*expensive*) The Hilton _____.

3 The beaches in England aren't as dirty as they used to be.
  (*clean*) _____.

4 Rian's restaurant isn't as expensive as Brown's.
  (*cheap*) Rian's restaurant _____.

5 The weather this week isn't as bad as it was last week.
  (*bad*) Last week _____.

b) [🔊 20.1] Listen and check your answers.

3 a) Choose the correct verb form and complete the sentences.

La Sagrada Familia in Barcelona

I (1) | am going
| to go   on holiday to Spain next week.
| going

The last time I (2) | have gone
| went   there was in 1994 and I
| have been going

(3) | was having
| have   a wonderful time. I (4) | have had
| had
| had
| was having

many holidays in Spain, usually by the sea, but

this time I (5) | am deciding   (6) | to visit
| have decided | visit
| decide | visiting

Barcelona for a week, and then travel south. As

soon as I (7) | arrive   I (8) | go
| will arrive | will go   to see some
| am arriving | going

buildings which (9) | designed
| was designed   by my favourite
| were designed

architect, Gaudí. When I was at college I

(10) | spend
| have spent   hours looking at books on
| used to spend

architecture and I really enjoy (11) | to walk
| walking
| walk

around cities looking at the buildings. I'd like

(12) | spend
| to spend   all my time visiting different cities
| spent

around the world but I can't. I have to work. If I

(13) | can   live my life again, I (14) | study
| could | will study
          | would study

architecture. Anyway, back to the holiday.

I (15) | am going
| will go   with my best friend Rose.
| go

I (16) | have been knowing
| know   Rose for over fifteen years.
| have known
| have been

We (17) | were   at school together in 1982. Rose is
| was being

a civil engineer, so she can teach me a lot about buildings. Yes, this will be my 'architecture'

holiday. I think it (18) | is
| will be   fun and I
| is being

(19) | will learn
| learn   a lot, too.
| to learn

b) [20.1]   Listen and check your answers.

VOCABULARY

4 Use *un-*, *dis-*, *in-* or *im-* to make the opposites of these words.

1 happy   *unhappy*
2 possible   _____
3 agree   _____
4 safe   _____
5 tidy   _____
6 comfortable   _____
7 necessary   _____
8 popular   _____
9 lucky   _____
10 complete   _____

5 Use *-ion* or *-ment* to change these words from verbs to nouns.

1 develop   *development*
2 educate   _____
3 excite   _____
4 decide   _____
5 discuss   _____
6 enjoy   _____
7 examine   _____

6 Complete the crossword.

ACROSS

1 a person who writes music
7 Have you heard the weather _____ for tomorrow?
8 a person who steals things
10 opposite of *safe*
12 Let's go to an ——— gallery.
13 Have you seen the head_____ in today's newspaper?
15 John's happy because he _____ his exams.
16 I _____ a football match on TV last night.

DOWN

2 a person who plays a musical instrument
3 Do you _____ golf?
4 opposite of *tidy*
5 Can you _____ after the children for me?
6 Can you _____ me $5 until tomorrow, please?
9 opposite of *generous*
11 I had to walk because my car _____ down.
14 Mary's going _____ with Peter now.

LISTENING

7 a) What was the best holiday you ever had?

b) [20.3]   Listen to Bob talking about his best holiday. Which of these sentences are correct?

1 Bob was a student. ____
2 Bob flew to Turkey with some friends. ___
3 That was the only holiday Bob has had. ___
4 It was a cheap holiday. ___

c) Listen again and write the questions for these answers.

1 *Who did Bob go to Turkey with*?
He went with three friends from university.
2 _____?
They travelled in an old Volkswagen van.
3 _____?
Because he was working every night and he didn't study.
4 _____?
They stayed in Turkey for two months.

d) Listen again and answer these questions.

1 How old was Bob when he went to Turkey?
He was twenty.
2 Why did he get a job in a pub?
_____.
3 Where did they sleep?
_____.
4 Did they always have enough money for food?
_____.
5 Did the van break down?
_____.
6 Did they get angry when things went wrong?
_____.
7 What three activities did they do?
_____.

WRITING

Linking words

8 a) Circle the correct linking word.

Dear Gerhard,

I'm very sorry I couldn't come to your leaving party last night, (1) so/but/and I had a terribly sore throat (2) so/but/because I went to the doctor's. I had to wait two hours to see her (3) when/although/because a lot of other people were there (4) and/so/but they all had sore throats, too. (5) However/Although/When, the doctor gave me some medicine (6) and/but/when I feel fine again.

I hope you like your new job (7) when/and/so you get back to Germany. (8) Finally/When/So you have time please write and give me your new address (9) so/ and/however I'll write to you.

I think we all enjoyed our English class (10) because/then/and I hope we have all passed the exam. (11) So/And/However, I don't think Ivan wanted to pass his exam (12) but/so/because he wants to stay in London with his new girlfriend Sonia. If he fails, his company will tell him to stay (13) but/so/and take the exam again!

I'm going to stay in London for three more weeks (14) because/so/but I can visit all the places I haven't seen. (15) When/Then/Because I'm going back to Bucharest.

I hope you had a great party (16) so/and/because I hope we can meet again some day in the future. I'll miss everyone I met at the school (17) and/so/but it'll be nice to see my family again.

Best wishes
Alex

b) [🔊 20.4]   Listen and check your answers.

DICTATION

Sound and spelling: *g*

9 a)[🔊 20.5]   Listen and write the sentences.

1 _____.
2 _____.
3 _____.
4 _____.

b) [🔊 20.6]   We can pronounce the letter *g* in different ways, /g/ or /dʒ/ or it can be a silent letter. Listen and write the words in the correct box.

design   luggage   giant   Gillian   garden   pig
gun   bright   orange   judge   page   fog
change   again   ugly   light   large   fridge
George   Gary   bridge   goal   agent   foreign

Silent 'g'	/g/	/dʒ/
design	luggage	giant

Tapescripts

Unit 1

RECORDING 3

BEN: Excuse me is this seat free?
SUE: Yes, it is.
BEN: May I sit here?
SUE: Yes.
BEN: Thank you. The café's always busy on the first day of term. My name's Ben, by the way.
SUE: Hello, Ben. My name's Sue. Are you studying here?
BEN: No. I teach business studies to the first year students.
SUE: Oh, really! That's what I came here to study, business. Am I in your class?
BEN: Just a minute, I've got the names here. What's your surname?
SUE: Burnet, Sue Burnet.
BEN: Is that B E R?
SUE: No. It's B U R N E T.
BEN: Oh right... Yes, here's your name, you're in my class.
SUE: Oh, great. Can you tell me where the room is?
BEN: Yes. Just let me check ... erm. Ah, here it is, room two F. That's on the second floor, and it's the fourth door on the right. The class starts at nine thirty.
SUE: Second floor. Fourth door on the right?
BEN: Yes, that's right. It's easy to find. So Sue, why are you studying business?
SUE: Because I'd really like to have my own company one day.
BEN: And what kind of business are you interested in?
SUE: Well, buying and selling motorbikes.
BEN: Motorbikes! That's interesting.
SUE: Yes, I know it's unusual for a woman, but I love them.
BEN: Me, too. Oh, dear. Look at the time. It's twenty-five to ten. We're late for our first class.
SUE: Room two F is it?
BEN: Don't worry. Just follow me.
SUE: Oh, thanks.
BEN: Come on.

Unit 3

RECORDING 2

INTERVIEWER: Anne, can I ask you how old you are?
ANNE: Yes, I'm twenty-six.
INTERVIEWER: Do you have any brothers or sisters?
ANNE: Yes, I'm the youngest of three children. I have a brother who is five years older and a sister who is eight years older than me.
INTERVIEWER: Do you think that being the first, second or third child in a family makes any difference to a child's personality?
ANNE: Yes, I do really. My sister is more serious than I am. She really studied a lot at school. She didn't have much fun. I'm more easy-going. I don't worry about things and I'm not very ambitious. I'm very different from my sister, but my brother is more like me. He's very friendly and fun to be with. But he is more independent than I am. I need people more than he does.
INTERVIEWER: Do you have any brothers and sisters, Brian?
BRIAN: No, I'm an only child.
INTERVIEWER: Did you want brothers and sisters when you were younger?
BRIAN: Oh, yes. I wanted a brother very much.
INTERVIEWER: Do you think being an only child made a difference to your personality?
BRIAN: That's a difficult question. Um, I don't really know. Erm, I think I'm generous, I'm a bit quiet but I like being with other people. Maybe that's because I didn't have any brothers and sisters.
INTERVIEWER: Did you have a happy childhood?
BRIAN: Oh, yes. I was very happy.
INTERVIEWER: Brian, you're not married now, but er would you like your own family one day?

BRIAN: Yes, yes I would. I'd like to have three or four children. But not yet, I'm only twenty-three.
INTERVIEWER: Gillian, you're a middle child, is that correct?
GILLIAN: Yes, I have a younger brother and an older sister.
INTERVIEWER: When you were young, was it easy to be the middle child?
GILLIAN: Yes. It was OK. I think my older sister had a more difficult time than I did, because she had to help Mum when Ben was a baby. I only played with him.
INTERVIEWER: Do you think being the middle child makes a difference to your personality?
GILLIAN: Perhaps. My sister gets angry quickly and my brother doesn't like being alone. I'm more easy-going, I think, fun-loving.

Unit 4

RECORDING 1

INTERVIEWER: Many people have parts of their bodies which they don't like. Today we're going to interview two people who are often in front of a camera. First is Mike, an actor who does a lot of television work. Mike, you are in front of cameras every day. Do you feel happy about being photographed?
MIKE: Well, being in front of a camera is my job, but there are things about my body which I don't really like very much. For example, I'm not very tall. I'd love to be twelve centimetres taller, and I think my ears are a bit big.
INTERVIEWER: And what do you like about your body?
MIKE: People say I've got nice eyes. Yes, my eyes are all right. The shape of my face is OK, I suppose, and I quite like my nose. It's like my father's nose, straight and quite small.
INTERVIEWER: Thank you, Mike. And now to you, Debbie. You're a model. People think you've got a perfect body. Do you agree?
DEBBIE: Oh, no! Definitely not! I think my mouth's too big. I don't like my teeth, they're too big. I've also got big feet, and it's difficult to find nice shoes in big sizes.
INTERVIEWER: Well, a lot of women would love to have your mouth and teeth. What do you like about your body?
DEBBIE: Well, I'm tall and I like being tall. I like my hair because it's easy to take care of. I just wash it and then leave it, and it always looks OK. I think my legs are all right. They're long and I like the shape. I've got quite a small waist which I like. That's about all really.
INTERVIEWER: Thank you very much, Mike and Debbie. It's nice to know that even very good-looking people have things they don't like about themselves.

Unit 6

RECORDING 2

Sophie Drew left home two years ago. She's at university in the North of England.

Well, I think the food I eat is fine really, but I know my Mum thinks it's terrible. She thinks that you need to eat fruit and vegetables every day, and I don't. Some days I just have a hamburger at lunch and a sandwich in the evening. I don't get ill very often, so my diet isn't too bad, but I like going home some weekends just to get some good home cooking.

Sylvia Stapleton is studying ballet in London.

Oh, dear. I hate talking about my diet. I know it's not good, but it's impossible to dance after a big meal, so I don't eat much before eight in the evening. I hope my parents don't hear this. I have a banana at about six in the morning when I wake up, then I only drink water or orange juice during the day, but in the evening I have a meal. Sometimes fish, sometimes a cheese salad, but I never eat meat. It isn't much is it? My Dad always says I look too thin, so when I go home to visit, I wear big sweaters and I eat a lot so that he won't worry about me.

David Conroy is studying engineering in Scotland.

I eat well really. I enjoy cooking and I try lots of new recipes. I only have a light meal for lunch, something like a salad or a sandwich, but in the evening I usually have a two course meal. For example, last night I made bacon pasta, a green salad, and for dessert I had some Italian ice-cream and fruit salad. It was lovely.

Unit 8

RECORDING 3

INTERVIEWER:	Mandy, you're a junior doctor. What does that mean?
MANDY:	It means I've finished medical school, and this is my first job in a hospital. This is where we really learn to be doctors.
INTERVIEWER:	We hear a lot about junior doctors working long hours every day. Is this true?
MANDY:	Yes, it really is. The rule is that we shouldn't work more than eighty-three hours in one week, but I sometimes work a hundred hour week. It's really tiring. The first weekend I worked in this hospital I had eighty calls on my bleeper, I worked from nine am on Friday to five pm on Monday and I only had a few hours sleep.
INTERVIEWER:	Do you have to carry your bleeper with you all the time?
MANDY:	No, not in my free time, but when I'm on duty, the hospital can call me at home at any time, day or night. The bleeper usually starts bleeping just when I'm sitting down to eat, or getting into the bath, or going to bed.
INTERVIEWER:	Well, do you earn a lot of money?
MANDY:	Junior doctors don't get a lot of money. When I work overtime, I get four pounds twenty two p per hour. The people who clean the hospital at night get more money than I do.
INTERVIEWER:	What happens to you when you work more than eighty hours in a week?
MANDY:	Well, I'm frightened of making a mistake. Someone could die if I make a mistake. And when you're tired your brain doesn't work very well. Another thing is well, you aren't always polite to people. It's not because you enjoy being impolite, it's just that you're too tired. Sometimes I get a call in the middle of the night when I'm asleep, and it's not important, the patient just needs an aspirin. And then I get a bit annoyed.
INTERVIEWER:	Are you married?
MANDY:	Em... I think I am. I haven't seen my husband for two weeks. But it's OK. He understands. He's a junior doctor, too!

Unit 9

RECORDING 4

Linda

Well, I chose this house because I love the sea so much, and I can see it from the front bedroom window. The house is quite small really. It only has one bedroom so when friends come to stay they have to sleep in the living room.

I have to have a car because there aren't any shops or other houses near me, but I like that. People ask me if I get frightened, and when there's a bad storm it is a bit frightening, but I usually phone my father. He talks for hours on the phone, so I forget about the storm and it's usually finished before my father stops talking!

I lived in London for many years when I was at art school, before I bought this house, but I couldn't live in a city now. Cities are just too noisy, too dirty and there are too many people.

I'm an artist, and I love painting the sky and the sea, so this place is perfect for me, just perfect.

Graham

I work in a bank in the city and I bought this flat in 1992. I bought it because it's near the city centre. I don't have a car. But because I live so close to shops, cinemas, discos, restaurants, I can walk from my flat to anywhere I want to go. It's great. I love it.

It's got two bedrooms, a big kitchen, a living room and a bathroom.

The only problem is that I'd like to have a dog, and I think you really need a garden if you have a dog. It's very difficult to find a flat with a garden in the city. So if I ever get rich, I'll buy one of the terraced houses in the next street. They're very expensive, but they have gardens. Um, yes, I'd like a garden, I really would.

Unit 12

RECORDING 3

POLICEWOMAN:	Mrs Daniels can you tell us exactly what happened?
MRS DANIELS:	Well, I left the house at eight and took the two older children to school. After that I went to the shops with William, my baby, and bought a few things for dinner this evening. Then I went home. I think it was about ten when I got back home. I was walking to the front door when I saw a man in the house. The front door has a window in it. He was in the hall. I was really frightened and I started screaming. The burglar heard me and he ran out of the back door. I quickly picked up William and ran to the back garden. My neighbour, Mrs Stevens, heard me screaming and she came running out of her house. When I got round to the back of the house, I saw the man jump over the wall, and he ran off down the road. I only saw the back of him, but Mrs Stevens saw his face. Then I just started crying, I was so frightened. Mrs Stevens took me into her house, called you and my husband. Then she made me a cup of tea.
POLICEWOMAN:	So you haven't been in the house yet? You don't know if he took anything?
MRS DANIELS:	No, I couldn't go in the house. Not with the baby. And I don't want to go in until my husband gets here.
POLICEWOMAN:	I quite understand Mrs Daniels. You've had a terrible shock.

Unit 14

RECORDING 2

INTERVIEWER:	Could you tell me your name, please.
MARC:	Marc Lacey.
INTERVIEWER:	What entertainment do you enjoy, Marc?
MARC:	Erm, theatre and music really. Those are my main interests.
INTERVIEWER:	Do you go to concerts?
MARC:	Yes, I do. Almost every night.
INTERVIEWER:	Every night?
MARC:	Nearly every night.
INTERVIEWER:	That's expensive, isn't it?
MARC:	Not if you're a musician who's playing in the concert.
INTERVIEWER:	Oh. You play in a band. Now I understand. What's the name of your group?
MARC:	Agony.
INTERVIEWER:	That's a rock group, isn't it?
MARC:	Well, yes. We play rock and reggae.
INTERVIEWER:	Er, what's your name, please.
CAROL:	Carol Barnes.
INTERVIEWER:	How do you enjoy yourself in the evenings, Carol?
CAROL:	That's an easy question. I love reading and music.
INTERVIEWER:	What kind of music do you like?
CAROL:	Most of the time I listen to classical music but I like all kinds of music. Well, not all. I don't like opera.
INTERVIEWER:	And your favourite author?
CAROL:	At the moment it's Isabel Allende.
INTERVIEWER:	She comes from Chile, doesn't she?
CAROL:	Yes. My idea of good entertainment is to sit by the fire, with some Chopin playing on my stereo system, reading one of her books. I think she's the most exciting writer we have at the moment.

INTERVIEWER:	Excuse me, what's your name, please.
SALLY:	Sally Davidson.
INTERVIEWER:	What's your favourite entertainment?
SALLY:	Well, I spend as much time as possible in art galleries. But only if they're free!
INTERVIEWER:	There aren't many free art galleries now, are there?
SALLY:	No. There used to be a lot in this city, but not now.
INTERVIEWER:	Are you an artist?
SALLY:	No, I'm not, but my father is a sculptor. A very poor one!
INTERVIEWER:	And what do you do for entertainment when the galleries aren't open?
SALLY:	I don't have enough money to go to the cinema, but I like films. And I have a friend who has a video recorder. He's very kind and I watch videos with him a lot.

Unit 16

RECORDING 2

Here is the news.

Two brothers, Sam and Toby Dayton, were saved earlier today when their tree house caught fire. Their mother, Mrs Jane Dayton, was cooking lunch in the kitchen when she saw smoke coming from the tree in the garden. She ran outside, climbed the tree and helped her sons to safety. The two boys were taken to hospital for a check-up but they weren't badly injured and they were sent home. When she was interviewed, Mrs Dayton said she had never climbed a tree before in her life, and she hoped she never had to climb another one again.

A five-year-old girl's life was also saved earlier today by her pet dog. Janice Sotherby was playing near the River Cam when her ball fell into the water. She tried to get the ball but she fell into the river. Her pet dog Rover jumped into the water and pulled Janice to the side and she climbed to safety. Janice was not hurt, but her mother, who was looking the other way at the time, was taken to hospital. She was suffering from shock.

The local beach was closed to the public this afternoon after twenty people were stung by jellyfish. The last time Braystones beach was closed because of jellyfish was in 1985. The police said people should not go in the sea. The twenty people who were stung were taken to hospital for treatment.

Unit 17

RECORDING 1

INTERVIEWER:	Most people love Christmas, Jeff. Why don't you?
JEFF:	Well, I disagree! I think most people hate Christmas but they feel they have to enjoy it.
INTERVIEWER:	But why don't you enjoy it?
JEFF:	I remember when I was a child, I loved getting presents on Christmas morning, but I also remember a lot of family arguments. We had a quiet family life all year, then suddenly the house was full of aunts, uncles, cousins and grandparents, all arguing. It was terrible. So, I didn't enjoy it even when I was a child.
INTERVIEWER:	What did they argue about?
JEFF:	Anything and everything! They argued about helping with the cooking. They argued about helping with the washing up. They argued about tidying up. Anything really. Then everyone used to eat too much and feel sick.
INTERVIEWER:	But don't you think there's a lovely feeling everywhere – the Christmas trees, the lights in the streets, the shop windows full of presents?
JEFF:	No, I don't! People in shops are really bad-tempered at Christmas. They push and shout. And the presents, well! I think it's very sad that people spend a lot of money on presents that no one wants. Every year I get shaving cream from my Aunt Lucy. And I've got a beard. I've had this beard since I was twenty and that was ten years ago.
INTERVIEWER:	Oh, I see your point. Well, thank you for talking to us. I won't say Merry Christmas to you, Jeff. I'll just hope you have a nice quiet time. What are going to do this year?
JEFF:	Oh, the same as I usually do. I'm working at the hospital. I'm a nurse. I like spending Christmas Day with people I don't know very well. It's much better than listening to the family shouting at each other.

Unit 19

RECORDING 1

The worst accident I've had was when I went skiing for the first time!

It happened when I was living in Canada. Some friends of mine decided that I should learn to ski and they asked me to go to a ski resort with them one Saturday. I enjoyed the drive to the mountains very much, but that was the only thing that I enjoyed that day. I remember it was one of the worst days of my life.

I didn't have my own equipment so I had to hire skis and boots. They didn't really fit me very well. I didn't have enough money to get the right jacket and trousers so I wore my jeans and three sweaters. Anyway, my friends took me to the 'nursery' ski slope where all the children were skiing. Paul told me to point my feet together and push with the ski poles. That was all I had to do, he said. Then my friends went to the advanced ski slopes and said they would come back for me in the afternoon.

I fell down again and again. It was very embarrassing. All the children could ski perfectly. I was the only one on the nursery slope who couldn't ski.

At one point when I fell down, a little girl, who was about four, skied into my leg. She was skiing without any poles and waving to her father. She didn't see me sitting in the snow. The poor little girl skied into my knee and went right over my legs. I was so worried about the little girl that I didn't feel any pain in my leg. The little girl's father came quickly. He saw some blood in the snow and thought his daughter was bleeding, but she was OK, she wasn't hurt. Then I looked at my leg. The blood was mine, and a lot of it wasn't in my body! It was in the snow.

The worse thing of all was in the emergency department at the hospital. The nurse had to cut my jeans to get them off. My favourite jeans! I was in hospital for a week. That was my first and my last skiing holiday.

Unit 20

RECORDING 3

Oh, the best holiday of my life was a holiday I had in Turkey when I was twenty. Three of my friends from university were driving to Turkey in an old Volkswagen van for their summer holidays, and they asked me to go with them. I had very little money so before university finished for the summer break I worked every evening in a pub. I earned enough money to go on the holiday. We didn't need a lot of money because we planned to sleep in the van, but we needed money for food, drink and petrol. Because I was working every evening I didn't study for my end of year examinations. I failed my exams, but I had a fantastic holiday. Lots of things went wrong with the van and it broke down three or four times. But somehow we managed to get to Turkey and we stayed there for two months! I can remember wonderful evenings walking on the beach, or swimming as the sun went down, or playing football with some Turkish boys from the village. We had to find the cheapest food, the cheapest drinks, the cheapest everything because we had very little money. On one or two days we didn't eat anything, because we had no money. But, I really think it was because we had so little money that we had such a good time. We laughed about everything that went wrong. Even when the van broke down we saw the funny side of it and laughed. I have had a few holidays since then, but that one, the holiday in Turkey, was the cheapest and the best. It really was great.